MMEDIA 2020

The Twelfth International Conferences on Advances in Multimedia

February 23 - 27, 2020

Lisbon, Portugal

MMEDIA 2020 Editors

Michele Covell, Google Research, USA

Printed from e-media with permission by:

Curran Associates, Inc.
57 Morehouse Lane
Red Hook, NY 12571

Some format issues inherent in the e-media version may also appear in this print version.

Printed with permission by Curran Associates, Inc. (2020)

International Academy, Research, and Industry Association (IARIA)
412 Derby Way
Wilmington, DE 19810

Phone: (408) 893-6407
Fax: (408) 527-6351

petre@iaria.org

Additional copies of this publication are available from:

Curran Associates, Inc.
57 Morehouse Lane
Red Hook, NY 12571 USA
Phone: 845-758-0400
Fax: 845-758-2633
Email: curran@proceedings.com
Web: www.proceedings.com

Table of Contents

MMEDIA 2020

Forward

The Twelfth International Conference on Advances in Multimedia (MMEDIA 2020), held between February 23-27, 2020 in Lisbon, Portugal, continued a series of events presenting recent research results on advances in multimedia, mobile and ubiquitous multimedia and to bring together experts from both academia and industry for the exchange of ideas and discussion on future challenges in multimedia fundamentals, mobile and ubiquitous multimedia, multimedia ontology, multimedia user-centered perception, multimedia services and applications, and mobile multimedia.

The rapid growth of information on the Web, its ubiquity and pervasiveness makes the www the biggest repository. While the volume of information may be useful, it creates new challenges for information retrieval, identification, understanding, selection, etc. Investigating new forms of platforms, tools, principles offered by Semantic Web opens another door to enable humans programs, or agents to understand what records are about, and allows integration between domain-dependent and media-dependent knowledge. Multimedia information has always been part of the Semantic Web paradigm, but requires substantial effort to integrate both.

The new technological achievements in terms of speed and the quality of expanding and creating a vast variety of multimedia services like voice, email, short messages, Internet access, m-commerce, to mobile video conferencing, streaming video and audio.

Large and specialized databases together with these technological achievements have brought true mobile multimedia experiences to mobile customers. Multimedia imply adoption of new technologies and challenges to operators and infrastructure builders in terms of ensuring fast and reliable services for improving the quality of web information retrieval.

Huge amounts of multimedia data are increasingly available. The knowledge of spatial and/or temporal phenomena becomes critical for many applications, which requires techniques for the processing, analysis, search, mining, and management of multimedia data.

We welcomed academic, research and industry contributions. The conference had the following tracks:

- Multimedia content-based retrieval and analysis
- Multimedia applications
- Social Big Data in Multimedia

We take here the opportunity to warmly thank all the members of the MMEDIA 2020 technical program committee, as well as all the reviewers. The creation of such a high quality conference program would not have been possible without their involvement. We also kindly thank all the authors who dedicated much of their time and effort to contribute to MMEDIA 2020. We truly believe that, thanks to all these efforts, the final conference program consisted of top quality contributions.

We also thank the members of the MMEDIA 2020 organizing committee for their help in handling the logistics and for their work that made this professional meeting a success.

We hope that MMEDIA 2020 was a successful international forum for the exchange of ideas and results between academia and industry and to promote further progress in the field of multimedia. We also hope that Lisbon, Portugal provided a pleasant environment during the conference and everyone saved some time to enjoy the historic charm of the city.

MMEDIA 2020 Chairs

MMEDIA Steering Committee
Jean-Claude Moissinac, TELECOM ParisTech, France
Daniel Thalmann, Nanyang Technological University, Singapore

MMEDIA Industry/Research Advisory Committee
Giuseppe Amato, CNR-ISTI, Italy

MMEDIA 2020

Committee

MMEDIA Steering Committee

Jean-Claude Moissinac, TELECOM ParisTech, France
Daniel Thalmann, Nanyang Technological University, Singapore

MMEDIA Industry/Research Advisory Committee

Giuseppe Amato, CNR-ISTI, Italy

MMEDIA 2020 Technical Program Committee

Manuel Alberto M. Ferreira, University Institute of Lisbon - School of Technology and Architecture, Portugal
Pedro A. Amado Assunção, Instituto de Telecomunicações|Politécnico de Leiria, Portugal
Giuseppe Amato, CNR-ISTI, Italy
José António Filipe, University Institute of Lisbon - School of Technology and Architecture, Portugal
Hugo Barbosa, Lusofona University of Porto / Faculty of Engineering of the University of Porto, Portugal
Fernando Boronat Seguí, Universitat Politecnica de Valencia-Campus de Gandia, Spain
Dumitru Dan Burdescu, Universityof Craiova, Romania
Baoyang Chen, Central Academy of Fine Arts, Beijing, China
Trista Chen, Inventec Corporation, Taiwan
Maaike de Boer, TNO, Netherlands
Franca Debole, Institute of Information Science and Technologies - Italian National Research Council (ISTI-CNR), Pisa, Italy
Jana Dittmann, Otto-von-Guericke-University Magdeburg, Germany
Vlastislav Dohnal, Masaryk University, Brno, Czech Republic
Filiz Ersoz, Karabük University, Turkey
Taner Ersoz, Karabük University, Turkey
Tolga Genc, Marmara University, Turkey
Konstantinos Gkountakos, CERTH (Centre For Research & Technology Hellas) | ITI (Institute of Informatics), Greece
William Grosky, University of Michigan-Dearborn, USA
Jun-Won Ho, Seoul Women's University, South Korea
Yin-Fu Huang, National Yunlin University of Science and Technology, Taiwan
Dimitris Kanellopoulos, University of Patras, Greece
Sokratis K. Katsikas, Norwegian University of Science and Technology, Norway
Panos Kudumakis, Queen Mary University of London, UK
Fons Kuijk, Distributed andInteractive Systems - CWI, Amsterdam, Netherlands
Anthony Y. H. Liao, Asia University, Taiwan
Xin Liu, University of Oulu, Finland
S. Manoharan,University of Auckland, New Zealand
Dani Marfil Reguero, Universitat Politècnica de València, Spain

Copyright Information

AR Smart Home: a Smart Appliance Controller Using Augmented Reality Technology and a Gesture Recognizer

Sora Inomata
Department of Computer Science and Engineering,
Waseda University, Japan
email: masolainota@dcl.cs.waseda.ac.jp

Koya Iwase
Department of Computer Science and Engineering,
Waseda University, Japan
email: chocochan_i@dcl.cs.waseda.ac.jp

Kosuke Komiya
Department of Computer Science and Engineering,
Waseda University, Japan
email: kosukekomiya@dcl.cs.waseda.ac.jp

Tatsuo Nakajima
Department of Computer Science and Engineering,
Waseda University, Japan
email: tatsuo@dcl.cs.waseda.ac.jp

Abstract— **Recently, smart speakers have become commercially common operation methods for controlling home appliances, and they have solved some of the problems with remote control operations. However, smart speakers also have some problems. For example, it is difficult to use voice recognition in a noisy environment. In addition, it takes a long time to check the current status of home appliances because users have to ask their smart speakers questions or give commands and wait for answers. To investigate other remote operation methods, we propose AR Smart Home, which uses the augmented reality technology and gesture recognition technology. Through evaluating the prototype system, we found that operating home appliances with gestures and interacting with virtual 3D home appliances instead of the actual home appliances are acceptable in terms of usability.**

Keywords- Augmented Reality; Smart Home; Universal Control

I. Introduction

Recently, new information technologies have been developed to make our daily lives more comfortable and reduce our levels of stress. In particular, technologies based on the Internet of Things enable us to access various devices over the Internet. For example, one of the major changes in our daily lives is how to operate home appliances. Until now, we have operated various home appliances using various remotes. However, in such an environment, multiple remotes are scattered in the room, and users may lose track of where a required remote control is. In addition, since each remote control may have different operation methods, users need to learn each operation method and use it properly. A common remote control operation method is pushing buttons, but there are new operation methods; for example, Siri Remote [1] can operate an Apple TV [2] to access some video content. Users can move a cursor on the display or select something by touching or sliding on the flat panel of Siri Remote. Recently, smart speakers, such as Google Home [3] and Amazon Echo [4] have solved the problem of having multiple remotes. By introducing these smart speakers in our home, we can operate various home appliances by voice command. However, due to the characteristics of smart speakers, it is difficult to operate them in noisy environments. In addition, when users check the current statuses of their home appliances, it takes a long time to activate their smart speakers by voice and wait for the answers. We propose a new home appliance operation method that can solve these problems.

In this paper, we propose Augmented Reality Smart Home, which uses the Augmented Reality (AR) technology and gesture recognition technology. With AR Smart Home, it is possible to manipulate home appliances through gestures by interacting with 3D virtual objects corresponding to home appliances displayed in the room. In addition, users can recognize the current status of various home appliances by looking at how the 3D virtual objects are operating. In this paper, we evaluate the operation methods of various home appliances using augmented reality and gestures via the prototype application.

We conducted a user study to evaluate AR Smart Home using the prototype application. We found that the augmented reality technology and a gesture recognition technology for home appliance operation are acceptable in terms of usability. We also found that visual information displayed in personal space is preferred to be the minimum and that switching the operation target by gaze is intuitive. In addition, we found that assigning the same gestures to similar operations makes it easier to remember the gestures.

This paper is divided into the following sections. Section II shows the background and related work of our study. Section III explains the system architecture of AR Smart Home. Section IV describes the preliminary survey we conducted for investigating how to apply the augmented reality technology in AR Smart Home. Section V describes the design of AR Smart Home based on the results extracted from the preliminary survey in Section IV. Then, we explain our conducted user study for evaluating the prototype application in Section VI. Section VII shows the results and the analysis of user study. Finally, we conclude and describe the future work in Section VIII.

II. Background and Related Work

Recently, the augmented reality technology has been developed, and head-mounted displays, such as Microsoft HoloLens [5] and Magic Leap [6] have appeared. This technology is becoming more familiar in our lives. With the technology, virtual information can be expressed in the real world [12]. The development of this technology may greatly change the perceptions and experiences in our daily lives.

Kim et al. [13] proposed a universal remote controller that consists of a touch screen, buttons, a speaker, and a haptic dial that returns tactile feedback. The universal remote controller provides a simple and intuitive operation method for users using the menu screen displayed on the screen and tactile feedback on the dial. However, the shown scenario deals with only one home appliance, and it is difficult to switch the current operation target when users operate multiple home appliances.

Wang et al. [14] proposed a user-centered control system for home appliances that consists of a versatile infrared controller, a task-based web application and a server that communicates between the application and the controller. They conclude that control methods of home appliance may become more user-friendly and enjoyable by combining sensor technologies and other services.

There are other related studies using the augmented reality technology for home appliance control, such as [15] and [16]. However, few studies have evaluated applying the augmented reality technology to operation methods of home appliances in terms of usability.

III. System Architecture of AR Smart Home

This section describes the overall architecture of the AR Smart Home system.

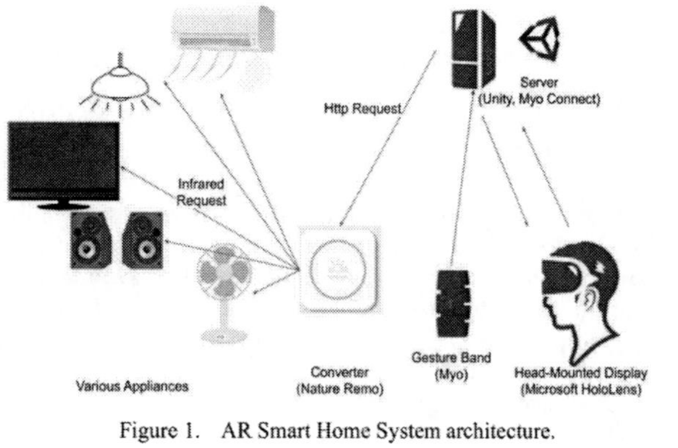

Figure 1. AR Smart Home System architecture.

Figure 1 shows the system architecture of AR Smart Home. The system uses Nature Remo [7] to operate home appliances by sending an HTTP request. The API of Nature Remo receives the HTTP request, and then Nature Remo sends preregistered infrared signals to home appliances. The system also includes Microsoft HoloLens to apply the augmented reality technology to display 3D virtual objects corresponding to each home appliance in the room. In addition, the system includes Myo [8] for gesture interaction with 3D virtual objects displayed in the room. By attaching Myo to the user's arm, various movements of the arm can be recognized. We implemented an application that organizes the processes of displaying 3D virtual objects through HoloLens, recognizing gestures through Myo and sending HTTP requests to Nature Remo. The application is implemented by Unity [9] and C#. The application uses the toolkit of Myo for the Myo gesture recognition and Mixed Reality Toolkit [10] for the HoloLens gesture recognition. The application also uses UnityWebSocket [11] for sending a HTTP Request. The sequence of the system is summarized as follows.

(1) The user performs a gesture in front of a 3D virtual object displayed through HoloLens.

(2) The application recognizes the gesture and sends a HTTP request to Nature Remo.

(3) Nature Remo receives the HTTP request and sends a preregistered infrared signal.

(4) The target home appliance receives the infrared signal and performs the defined operation.

In the early prototype, 3D home appliance objects corresponding to four home appliances (display, air conditioner, audio speaker, and lighting) are displayed in front of the user. The "air tap" gesture, which is bending the index finger in the user's sight, is implemented as an operation method activated by a gesture. Users "air tap" the 3D virtual object for it to display "Power On", "Volume Up", or other buttons above the object. Users "air tap" the button again to end the operation of the corresponding home appliance. Figure 2 shows the use of the early prototype.

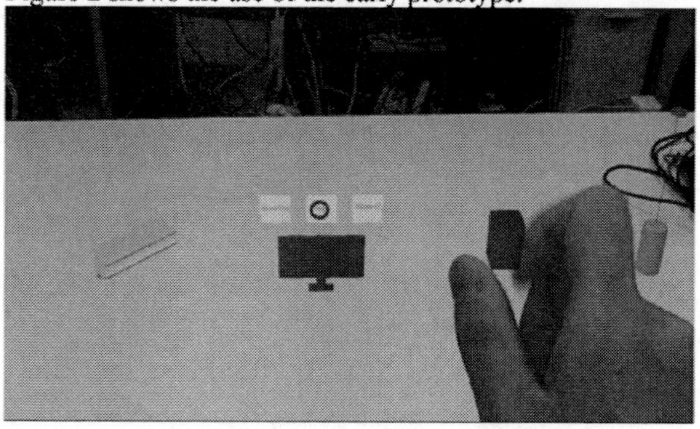

Figure 2. Using the early prototype application.

In Figure 2, the user is turning on the display by "air tapping" the button above the 3D virtual object displayed.

IV. Preliminary Survey

We conducted a preliminary survey to investigate how to apply augmented reality technology for AR Smart Home. This section describes our survey. We conducted the survey according to the following steps. First, an overview of AR Smart Home is given to participants and then they learned about the concept by watching a video and using the early prototype application. After that, participants answered questionnaires. Figure 3 shows a subject using the early prototype. In the preliminary survey, questionnaires were conducted on 78 people.

The contents of the questions are as follows.

(1) What kind of 3D virtual objects would be useful to represent home appliances?
(2) What functions would be useful on screens and operation methods?

Table 1 shows the answers to Question 1, and Table 2 shows the answers to Question 2.

Figure 3. Using the early prototype application in a preliminary survey.

TABLE I. THE ANSWERS TO QUESTION 1.

Answers	Num
3D virtual objects of home appliances	12
Animated characters with the same characteristics as home appliances	11
Other objects with characteristics similar to those of home appliances	5
3D virtual objects identified by color	3
Control panels of home appliances	3
Illustration of home appliance	2
Special tools and control panels based on fictional devices	2
Others	11

TABLE II. THE ANSWERS TO QUESTION 2.

Answers	Num
Feedback effects indicating control and appliance status	13
Large and simple screens for users to easily recognize objects	10
Customization function that allows you to move an object to a desired position	8
Screens where all objects are visible	2
Application of AI assistants	2
Others	10

In Question 1, we investigated what kind of 3D virtual objects are suitable to represent actual home appliances. The most common answer was "3D virtual objects of home appliances corresponding to actual home appliances" because users can easily understand what they are operating.

In Question 2, we investigated the required functions of the operation screen and operation method in AR Smart Home. The most common answers were "a function for displaying feedback on user's input and effects indicating the current status of home appliances" and "a function for placing 3D virtual objects in a desired position". There were also many responses, such as "3D virtual objects should be simple, large and easy to look at".

V. DESIGN OF AR SMART HOME

We improved the early prototype described in Section III in terms of the operation screen and the operation method based on the results of the preliminary survey described in Section IV. This section describes the improved design of AR Smart Home. It is assumed that home appliances operated with AR Smart Home can be operated with a remote control without touching the actual appliances, such as air conditioners, TVs, audio speakers, fans, lighting, and curtains. Figure 4 shows the use of the prototype application.

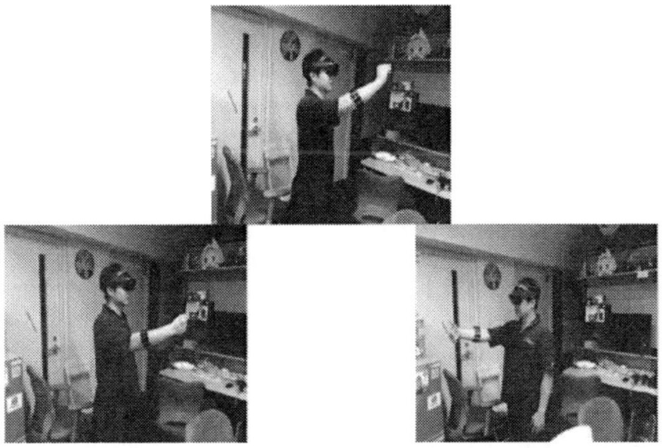

Figure 4. Using the prototype application.

Figure 5 shows a screen of the prototype application. Based on the results of the preliminary survey, we applied 3D virtual objects that are the same shape as the actual home appliances. These 3D virtual objects are white in their initial state.

Figure 5. A screenshot of the prototype application.

Figure 6. Placing a 3D virtual object.

The 3D virtual objects can be placed at the desired position by the user moving his or her hand and "air tapping" while putting the cursor on the target. In addition, the 3D virtual objects can be rotated by the user moving his or her hands and "air tapping" while putting the cursor on the target. Figure 6 shows how a user places a 3D virtual object.

Users can deliver commands to the target by performing gestures while placing the cursor displayed in the center of the sight on the target; then, the operation of the corresponding home appliance is completed. Table 3 shows the names of the gestures and their descriptions. Table 4 shows the correspondence of gestures to the operations of the home appliances.

Users can view the results of the operations and the current status of home appliances by seeing feedback. First, we describe the feedback related to the results of the operations. When the cursor is placed on the object and the object is selected as the operation target, the object changes from the original color to yellow. When the cursor is removed, the object returns to the original color. As shown in Table 4, "wave right" has the effect of increasing the volume or temperature of a target, and "wave left" has the effect of decreasing them. Therefore, when "wave right" is performed, the effect of red particles rising from the bottom of the target is displayed. Additionally, when "wave left" is performed, the effect of blue particles descending from the top of the target is displayed. Figure 7 shows the effects displayed when each gesture is performed. In Figure 7, the top figure shows the effect of raising the temperature on the air conditioner, and the bottom figure shows the effect of lowering the temperature on the air conditioner.

Next, we describe the feedback related to the current status of home appliances. As shown in Table 4, each home appliance can be turned on by performing "make a fist". So that users can immediately recognize whether the power is turned on by looking at the object, the object turned on by performing "make a fist" changes green. When the object is turned off by performing "make a fist", the object returns to the original color. An air conditioner has a cooling mode and a heating mode, and users cannot recognize which mode an air conditioner is in unless they feel the temperature on their skin. To make it easier to recognize which mode an air conditioner is in, the object becomes red when heating is set, and the object becomes blue when cooling is set.

In addition, the volume, fan speed, set temperature, and other states are displayed in text on the panel that is displayed above the object when the cursor displayed in the center of the sight is placed on the object.

TABLE III. GESTURES FOR OPERATING APPLIANCES.

Gestures	Descriptions
Make a fist	making a fist
Wave right	bending a wrist to the right
Wave left	bending a wrist to the left
Double-Tap	tapping an index finger and middle finger twice
Spread fingers	spreading fingers

TABLE IV. CORRESPONDENCE OF GESTURES AND OPERATIONS.

Appliances	Operations	Gestures
Air Conditioner	turning on the power	Make a fist
	raising the temperature	Wave right
	lowering the temperature	Wave left
	switching mode (heating, cooling)	Spread fingers
	switching fan speed (low, medium, high)	Double-Tap
Television	turning on the power	Make a fist
	increasing the volume	Wave right
	decreasing the volume	Wave left
	switching to the next channel	Double-Tap
Audio Speaker	turning on the power	Make a fist
	increasing the volume	Wave right
	decreasing the volume	Wave left
Fan	turning on the power	Make a fist
	switching fan speed (low, medium, high)	Double-Tap
Lightning	brightening / darkening	Make a fist
Curtains	opening / closing	Make a fist

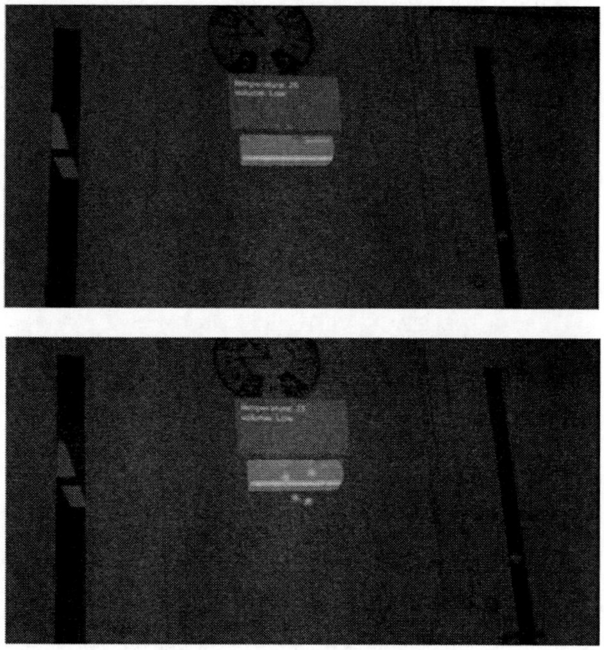

Figure 7. Effects of 3D virtual objects.

VI. USER STUDY

This section describes the user study we conducted to evaluate the prototype application. To evaluate the operation method using the augmented reality technology and gesture recognition technology, we conducted the user study without actually sending requests to home appliances. It was assumed that the home appliances were working as expected in the user study. In the user study, 10 participants aged 21-27 years participated. We conducted the user study according to the following steps. First, participants were told about the concept of this study and how to use the prototype application. After wearing the HoloLens and the Myo device, they customized the location of 3D virtual objects representing home appliances and operated the prototype application according to the given scenario. Finally, they answered a questionnaire using a 5-level Likert scale and answered questions in a semi-structured interview. To evaluate the usability of the system, we used the System Usability Scale (SUS) questionnaire [17]. The scenario given when participants operated the prototype application is as follows.

(1) You open the door of your room. Since the room is dark, you turn on the light in front of the door.
(2) Since you feel cold, you turn on the air conditioner and set the mode to the heating mode, the temperature to 20 degrees and the fan speed to medium.
(3) You want to watch a news program, so you turn on the TV and set the volume to 20.
(4) After finishing watching TV, you turn off everything and go to bed.

VII. RESULSTS AND ANALYSIS

This section describes the results of the user study described in Section VI and the analysis. We used the SUS questionnaire to evaluate the usability of the system. Table 5 shows the SUS items of the questionnaire. Figure 8 shows the average score for each question. The average SUS score was 70.0. According to [18], this average was within the acceptable range. We found that the usability of the prototype application was acceptable in terms of satisfaction.

TABLE V. SUS QUESTIONNAIRE ITEMS.

ID	Questionnaires
Q1	I think that I would like to use this system frequently.
Q2	I found the system unnecessarily complex.
Q3	I thought the system was easy to use.
Q4	I think that I would need the support of a technical person to be able to use this system.
Q5	I found the various functions in this system were well integrated.
Q6	I thought there was too much inconsistency in this system.
Q7	I would imagine that most people would learn to use this system very quickly.
Q8	I found the system very cumbersome to use.
Q9	I felt very confident using the system.
Q10	I needed to learn a lot of things before I could get going with this system.

TABLE VI. OUR QUESTIONNAIRE ITEMS.

ID	Questionnaires
Q11	Could you use the system without being stressed?
Q12	Is it suitable that the 3D home appliance object is displayed for interaction?
Q13	Is the feedback scale suitable?
Q14	Is it easy to switch home appliances by switching your gaze?
Q15	Did you use the gestures you learned as you intended?

In addition, we used some questions that we developed. Table 6 shows these items of the questionnaire. Figure 9 shows the average score for each question.

We provide the responses to each question that was raised in the interview after the questionnaire.

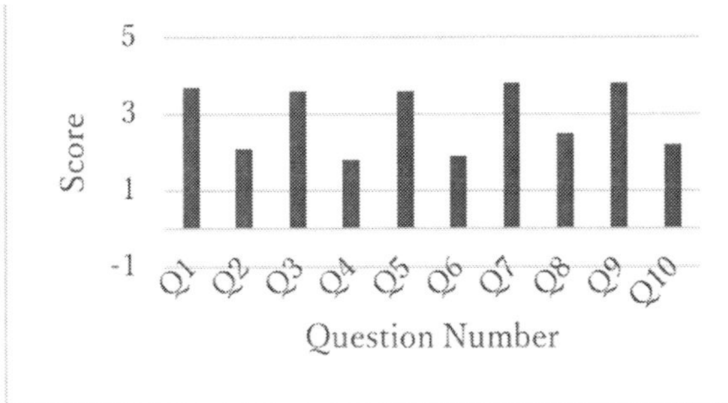

Figure 8. Scores for the SUS questionnaire.

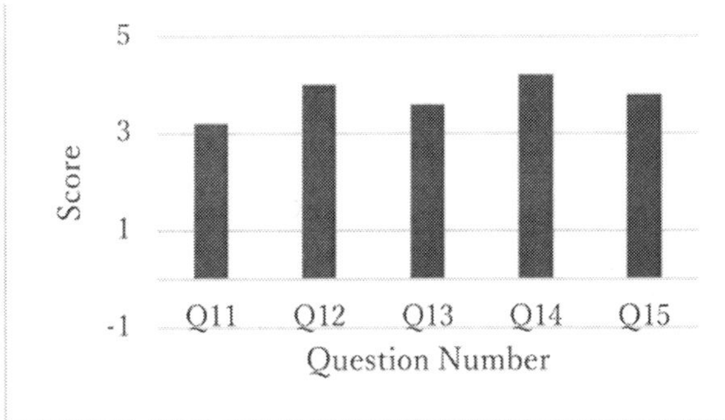

Figure 9. Scores for our questionnaire items.

In Q11, we investigated whether participants experienced stress when using the prototype application. Many of the participants who gave a relatively low score said, "There was something wrong due to the low recognition accuracy of Myo, but there was no stress about the use of gestures as operations if the accuracy was good." The system relies on the Myo function for gesture recognition, so it may be necessary to consider using another device to improve the accuracy of gesture recognition; however, we found that there is no stress in operating home appliances with gestures.

In Q12, we investigated whether it is appropriate to use 3D virtual objects representing home appliances instead of actual home appliances as the interaction target. The most common response was "It is intuitive and appropriate." In addition, there were responses, such as "The light object did not look like a light." and "It was difficult to adjust the line of sight to the light object compared to other objects because the light object was slender." It is necessary to improve the system by selecting objects in consideration of operability, such as selecting objects with wide shapes.

In Q13, we investigated whether the size scale of 3D virtual objects and the feedback displayed in the screen were appropriate. Most of the participants responded "I don't like displaying objects and feedback with ornate decorations in my room, so the simplicity of the system was just right." There was also the related response of "It is better to display them only when they are needed." We found that people usually prefer minimum visual information displayed in personal space, such as a room where people usually live.

In Q14, we investigated whether the method of switching the operation target by switching the line of sight is appropriate. Most of the participants responded that "It was easier to switch by line of sight than to change the remote control." There was also a response that "I would look at the operation target even if I use the remote control". We found that switching the operation target by gaze is intuitive.

In Q15, we investigated whether users can remember some gestures and use the gestures in their daily lives. Most of the participants responded that "If I get used to the system, I can handle gestures." There are similar operations in the operation of various home appliances, such as "turning on the power" and "raising and lowering something". We found that assigning the same gestures to similar operations makes it easier for users to remember and handle the gestures even if there are multiple gestures. There was also a response that "Human errors are likely to occur less often with gesture operations than with remote control operations." In remote control operations, various operations are performed by pressing a button. On the other hand, operation methods using several gestures can be easily distinguished from one other, and errors due to human recognition can be reduced.

In the interview, we also asked the question, "How would you place objects of home appliances in your room?". The most common response was "I would place them close together because when I look at them, I can operate various home appliances." One of the strengths of using augmented reality technology is that we can replace home appliances that have physical constraints with 3D virtual objects and place them at any position in the room without fear of them being lost.

VIII. Conclusions and Future Work

In this paper, we proposed AR Smart Home, which uses augmented reality technology and gesture recognition technology. We also evaluated the prototype application by a user study. Using gestures to operate home appliances is not stressful, and it is intuitive to interact with 3D virtual objects representing home appliances instead of actual home appliances, so the system is acceptable in terms of usability. We found that visual information displayed in personal space is preferred to be the minimum and that switching the operation target by gaze is intuitive. In addition, we found that assigning the same gestures to similar operations makes it easier to remember the operation gestures.

In the next step, we would like to remove various constraints in the current design. In the current design, gestures that can be recognized are limited to those recognized by Myo and HoloLens. By implementing other gestures, it will be possible to incorporate many other current remote-control operations. Then, it will be necessary to investigate how many gestures users can remember and use in daily life. In the research, we conducted the user study on the premise that users can use augmented reality technology and gesture recognition technology in their daily life. However, users have to equip some devices in order to use the system and it may limit the comfort. In this aspect, we should conduct more study. In addition, a function that can customize the correspondence between operations and gestures will be necessary. It may also be necessary for users to be able to define various shapes of objects for the operation target, as there are various shapes of home appliances. Depending on the user's mood, arranging various objects and creating a favorite room can make the prototype more enjoyable to use.

References

[1] Apple Inc, "Siri Remote – Apple", https://www.apple.com/shop/product/MQGD2LL/A/siri-remote, [Dec. 2019].

[2] Apple Inc, "TV - Apple", https://www.apple.com/tv/, [Dec. 2019].

[3] Google, "Google Home - Smart Speaker & Home Assistant – Google Store", https://store.google.com/product/google_home, [Dec. 2019].

[4] Amazon.com, Inc, "Amazon.com: Echo (2nd Generation) International Version – Charcoal Fabric: Amazon Devices", https://www.amazon.com/Echo-2nd-Generation-International-Version/dp/B075RSCZHD, [Dec. 2019].

[5] Microsoft, "Microsoft HoloLens | Mixed Reality Technology fo Bussiness", https://www.microsoft.com/en-us/hololens, [Dec. 2019].

[6] Magic Leap Inc, "Home | Magic Leap", https://www.magicleap.com/, [Dec. 2019].

[7] Nature Inc, "Nature Remo - Nature", https://nature.global/en/top, accessed [Dec. 2019].

[8] North Inc, "Welcome to Myo Support", https://support.getmyo.com/hc/en-us, [Dec. 2019].

[9] Unity Technologies, "Unity Real-Time Development Platform | 3D, 2D VR & AR Visualizations", https://unity.com/, [Dec. 2019].

[10] Microsoft, "Getting started with MRTK v2", https://docs.microsoft.com/ja-jp/windows/mixed-reality/mrtk-getting-started, [Jan. 2020].

[11] Unity Technologies, "UnityWebRequest", https://docs.unity3d.com/ja/2017.4/ScriptReference/Networking.UnityWebRequest.html/, [Jan. 2020].

[12] R. T. Azuma, "A Survey of Augmented Reality", Presence: Teleoperators and Virtual Environments, Vol. 6, Issue. 4, pp. 355–385, August 1997.

[13] L. Kim, W. Park, H. Cho, and S. Park, "An universal remote controller with haptic interface for home devices", 2010 Digest of Technical Papers International Conference on Consumer Electronics (ICCE), Las Vegas, pp. 209-210, 2010.

[14] D. Wang, K. Sugiura, and Y. Murase, "Design and Implementation of User-centered Home Appliance Controlling Service Environment", MoViD'14 Proceedings of Workshop on Mobile Video Delivery, No. 7, pp. 7:1-7:6, 2014.

[15] S. Mihara, K. Kawai, H. Shimada, and K. Sato, "EVANS 3: Home appliance control system with appliance authentication framework using Augmented Reality technology," 2013 IEEE 10th Consumer Communications and Networking Conference (CCNC), Las Vegas, pp. 849-850, 2013.

[16] R. Umeyama, and H. Suzuki, "iHAC: Smart appliance controller using AR technology," 2017 IEEE International Conference on Consumer Electronics (ICCE), Las Vegas, pp. 168-169, 2017.

[17] J. Brooke, "SUS : A quick and dirty usability scale", Taylor & Francis, Usability Evaluation in Industry, pp. 189-194, 1996.

[18] A. Bangor, P. Kortum, and J. Miller, "Determining what individual SUS scores mean: adding an adjective rating scale", Journal of Usability Studies, vol. 4, Issue. 3, pp. 114-123, May 2009

Safe Route Navigation Using Traffic Volume Estimated by Noise Data

Kenji Tsukamoto
Department of Computer Science and Engineering
Waseda University
Tokyo, JAPAN
e-mail: tenbook223@dcl.cs.waseda.ac.jp

Tatsuo Nakajima
Department of Computer Science and Engineering
Waseda University
Tokyo, JAPAN
e-mail: tatsuo@dcl.cs.waseda.ac.jp

Abstract—**The focus of this research is on the new possibilities of map-based pedestrian navigation applications. Currently, many map-based pedestrian navigations can only display the shortest path. However, it is not always appropriate for typical users. We propose a map-based pedestrian navigation application which presents a path that can reduce the fear of crime for the pedestrians. In other words, we propose a safe route navigator. Our research question is whether it is useful for the user that the application shows a safe path. We have created a prototype application that suggests a safe path and we also evaluate the usefulness of the application. We consider that a busy road is typically a safe road; however, estimating human density to indicate busy road is not easy. We propose a method of using the environmental noise as an easy way to estimate human density. Compared to the human density, the noise level can be easily measured. Then, we show that the proposed application can reduce the user's fear of crime. This means that future map-based pedestrian navigation application should show not only the shortest route but also a safe route.**

Keywords-route navigation; map application; safety; noise level.

I. INTRODUCTION

In recent years, smart devices, such as smartphones have become widespread. Further, various applications for these devices have become available. A map-based pedestrian navigation application is one of such applications. Many of such applications also have a route navigation function, which is used to find a route to the destination. Such map applications often suggest the shortest path to the user. However, valuable paths other than the shortest routes exist. For example, in railway transfer guidance in Japan, a route with a low fare or a route with a small number of transfers is displayed in addition to the shortest route. The research by Quercia et al. [1] presents a route navigation for walking. It proposes a beautiful route, a quiet route, and a happy route. Each route made a different impressions on the users.

In this paper, we created a map-based pedestrian navigation application that proposes routes with attributes other than shortest distance like Figure 1. The attribute we focused on is "Safety". In this paper, "Safety" means that the route is less susceptible to crime and does not take into account the dangers of traffic accidents. The research in [2] is as an example of a route guidance also focusing on "Safety". The authors created a system that uses a database that records the locations where crimes actually occurred. By using this database, they search for path with fewer crimes, and propose them to users. However, it is not easy to create a database of how many crimes have occurred in the past for all roads. According to Ohno et al. [3], the crime rate is low in Japan and the total amount of crime data is small. Therefore, it is difficult to accurately evaluate safety by simply comparing the number of crimes on each road. For this reason, in Japan, such an evaluation is often based on fear of crime and not the actual number of crimes. This paper also does not focus on the actual number of crimes but, rather, evaluates the perception of the crime rate.

Figure 1. Safe Route Navigation

We conducted two experiments. Experiment 1 shows the relationship between noise level and traffic in Tokyo, where noise level means the loudness of environmental noise. We studied people living in Tokyo and investigated the relationship between the noise level and the traffic. As a result of this study, we found that traffic is busy in areas where noise level is high. This result means that human density can be measured more easily.

Experiment 2 shows that the traffic information estimated in Experiment 1 is applicable, and that the route guidance that presents a busy route is useful. In experiment 2, we used the results of Experiment 1 to estimate the human density and created a map application that suggests a path with high traffic. The experiment consists of two sub-experiments. In Experiment 2-1, we showed that the sense of security estimated by the map application matches users' perceptions. Thus, the traffic information estimated by using the noise level is useful. In Experiment 2-2, we explored whether the safe path presented by the proposed application is useful for users and demonstrated the utility of this.

The structure of this paper is as follows. In Section II, we compare the proposed approach with existing research. In Section III, we show the usefulness of this research using assumed use cases. In Section IV, we survey people living in Tokyo and confirm that there is much traffic in a noisy place. Based on what is shown in Section IV, we create a map application that proposes a path with much traffic as a safe route, and show that it is useful for users in Section V. In Section VI, we present the findings and future prospects obtained through this study.

II. BACKGROUND

When do people feel fear of crime while walking? According to Ferraro et al. [4] and Braungart et al. [5], people feel this fear when there are no people around, although there are differences depending on gender and age. In isolated areas, fear increases because no other individuals are nearby to help if a person becomes the target of a crime. In other words, a place where there is little sense of fear of crime is a place that is easily noticeable, that is, a place with busy traffic. The fear of crime can be alleviated by navigating through a busy place.

To find busy places, pedestrian traffic data is needed. It is used in many situations, such as when the government decides on a city plan. On the other hand, it is difficult to actually measure pedestrian traffic, and data cannot be easily collected. Therefore, methods for estimating pedestrian traffic rather than actually measuring it have been studied.

One example of these studies is a method using Global Positioning System (GPS) [6]. GPS is a system that detects the position of a person using artificial satellites and can accurately acquire data on the position of the person. There is already research on using GPS for other services [7]. In this research, there is a method of measuring how many people are on each road and estimating the traffic volume of pedestrians. However, in urban areas with many high-rise buildings, it is difficult to receive radio waves from artificial satellites, and GPS may not provide accurate position. We can detect the number of devices that have GPS functions by this method, but it is not possible to determine the exact number of people. In addition, it is not possible to distinguish between people in a car and pedestrians. Therefore, it is difficult to estimate an accurate pedestrian traffic volume.

Another method of estimating pedestrian traffic is to use images or videos [8]. In this method, pedestrian traffic is estimated by analyzing road images or videos. The methods presented in [9]-[11] estimate the density of crowds; thus, we can estimate the pedestrian density even when there is a large amount of traffic. However, it is necessary to install a camera on the road to collect images or videos. It is difficult to collect images or videos because data cannot be collected from places where cameras are not installed. Thus, while information on pedestrian traffic is useful, it is difficult to estimate it. Therefore, we considered a method for estimating pedestrian traffic more easily and that is, the method using noise level.

It is easy to collect data of the noise level. For example, a smartphone has a built-in microphone. By using this, we can easily record and measure the volume of noise anywhere. By mapping this data, it is possible to know how much noise is generated in each place.

There is already a method for mapping noise data to a map. NoiseSpy [12] proposes two methods for displaying noise data on a map. The first method is called journey-based visualization, which displays the noise level along a specific route on the map. The second is city-based visualization, which divides the map into squares of a certain size and displays how much noise is generated in each area by color. By using these methods, noise data can be mapped.

We thought that pedestrian traffic volume could be estimated from mapped noise data. Many of the causes of noise in an urban area can be attributed to people. In other words, it can be estimated that a place in the city with many people has much noise. We can evaluate the noise level of each route by mapping the noise. We propose a method for estimating pedestrian traffic more easily by finding the relationship between noise level and pedestrian traffic.

III. SCENARIO AND REQUIREMENT ANALYSIS

In this section, we consider the situation in which the application that suggests a safe route, as proposed in this research, and determine if this suggestion is useful.

A. Scenario

Ms. Miya is a female university student. She was working on research at the university on a weekday at 7 p.m. She was tired of working at the university and decided to continue her work somewhere else. She searched for a new place to work. She found a new cafe approximately 10 minutes by foot from the university. She tried to go there by searching for a route to the café by using a map-based pedestrian navigation application. However, the road to the cafe was dark and quiet. She was worried about walking alone on the road and decided not to go to the cafe.

B. *Requirement Analysis*

The problem with this scenario is that the map-based pedestrian navigation application presented only the shortest route. If the application had presented a safe route, Ms. Miya would not have given up on going to the destination. Our application can present a safe route in addition to the shortest route. Therefore, it is possible to propose a route that allows users to reach the destination without fear of crime.

IV. EXPERIMENT 1

We conducted a survey to determine the relationship between noise data and pedestrian traffic in cities. The target city for the survey was Tokyo. To determine whether there are many people in a noisy place, we conducted a noise questionnaire for people living in Tokyo. We received 31 responses from people in their teens and 20s. Questionnaires used in the experiment are shown in Table 1. The results of the questionnaires are shown in Figure 2 and Figure 3.

TABLE I. QUESTIONS INCLUDED IN THE QUESTIONNARIE

Question number	Question
1	Where was the path noisy?
2	What was the source of noise?
3	At that time, how many people were there around you?

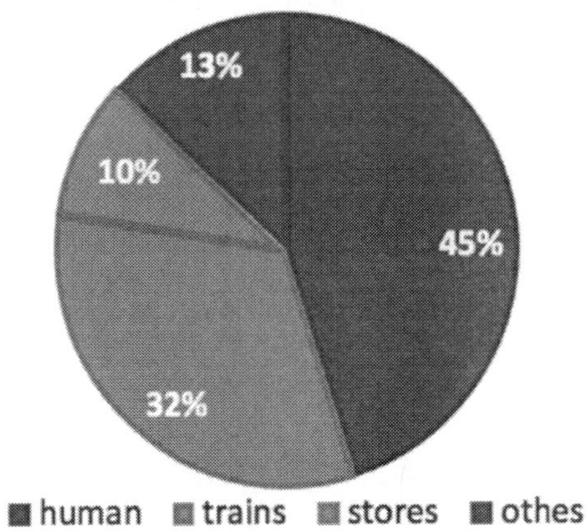

Figure 2. Results of the question 2

Figure 2 shows the responses to the question about the source of noise. The most common source of noise was from people, comprising 45 % of the total. The second most common cause was trains, comprising 32 % of the total. Other causes of noise included stores' advertisements, cars, factories, and large version. People were the most common cause of noise but made up less than half of the total noise.

Figure 3 shows how many people were around when the area was perceived as noisy. The largest number of respondents said that there were too many people to count, accounting for 61 % of the total. The second most common answer was approximately 10 people, making up 26 % of the total. The total of these two answers is 87 %. This result indicates that in more than 80 % of the places where noise occurred, there were more than 10 people in the surrounding area.

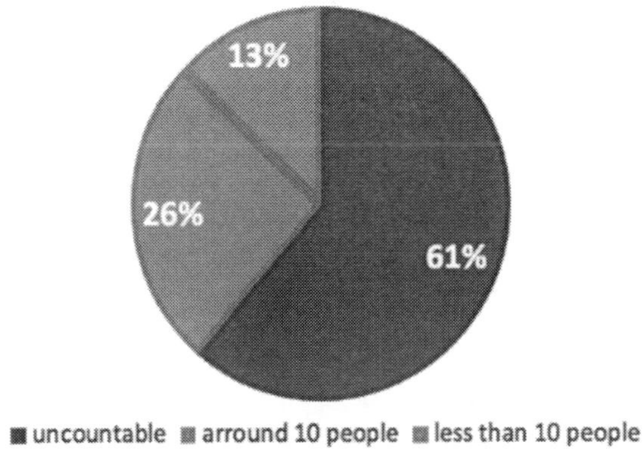

Figure 3. Results of the question 3

These results are summarized as follows. First, less than half of the urban noise was caused by people. On the other hand, it is clear that there are many people in areas that tend to be noisier. Therefore, it can be said that people do not cause much of the noise in the city, but pedestrian traffic is often found in a noisy place. In other words, we were able to show the relationship between noise level and pedestrian traffic, which is the purpose of this experiment.

V. EXPERIMENT 2

We created a map-based pedestrian navigation application that suggests routes that people can walk without fear of crime using pedestrian traffic estimates based on noise level. In this application, a place with much noise is treated as a busy place based on the result of Experiment 1. This application presents the user with a route through a noisy place, which is assumed to be a busy place and a place where one can walk without fear of crime. Figure 4 shows the processing flow of the application.

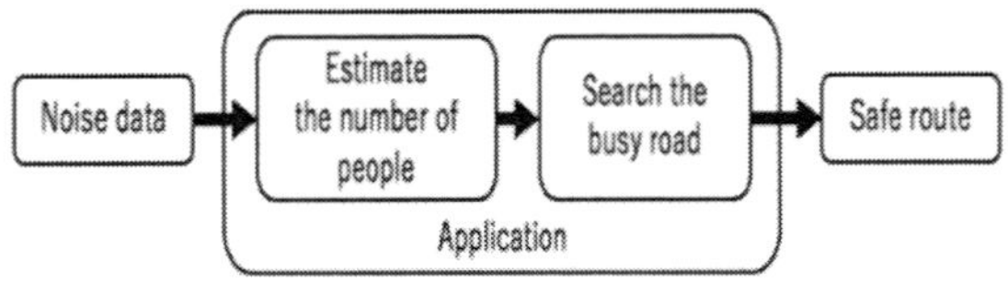

Figure 4. Processing flow of the map application

We conducted Experiment 2 in Takadanobaba in Tokyo shown in Figure 5. The size of the test area is approximately 200 m by 150 m. We divided the roads in the test area into 33 roads at each intersection. The noise was measured for each road and the pedestrian traffic volume was estimated. All measurements were taken between 7 p.m. and 8 p.m. Noise was measured using an iPhone. The application used for the measurement is a sound meter [13]. The measurement was performed at the midpoint of each road, and the average noise value for 30 seconds was calculated. The weather at the time of measurement at each point was cloudy and the wind speed was less than 5m; thus, we considered that the measurement value was not affected by the weather.

The experiment was divided into two parts. Experiment 2-1 presents the user with pictures of multiple roads that are judged to have different perceptions of safety depending on the application. We investigated whether there is actually a difference in the user's feeling of safety. In Experiment 2-2, the application presents the user with a fast route, a fast and safe route, and a safe route. We investigated whether the route indicated by this application is useful for users.

Figure 5. A map of evaluated area

The test subjects were 16 people in their 20s, of which 8 were male and 8 were female. Subjects are the same in Experiment 2-1 and Experiment 2-2.

A. *Map-based Pedestrian Navigation Application*

Our application presents the user with three routes: the shortest path, the shortest and safest path, and the safest path. We classified the road into three noise levels based on the noise measurements. Table 2 shows the noise level classification.

We set the coefficient *a* for each noise level and calculated the weighted distance L of each road based on this value and the actual road length l. The coefficient *a* increases as the noise decreases, which means that the weighted distance L increases as the road becomes quieter. In addition, by using the coefficient *n* that indicates how much emphasis is placed on security, it is now possible to search for routes that take both speed and safety into consideration and routes that take only safety into account. The coefficient *n* is 0 when searching for the shortest route, and increases as safety is emphasized. The formula used for the calculation is as follows. However, the route number is i and the noise level is j.

$$L_i = l_i \, (1 + a_j * n)$$

TABLE II. NOISE LEVEL CLASSIFICATION

Noise level	Volume	Number of roads classificated
Level 1	0-19Hz	11
Level 2	20-29Hz	10
Level 3	30-Hz	12

Our map application uses L to search the route from the current location to the destination. By searching for a route that minimizes L, it is possible to guide the route through a road with much noise (which also means that there is much traffic).

B. *Experiment 2-1*

The purpose of this experiment is to verify whether the degree of security estimated by the application is close to the user's perception. We presented three roads with different noise levels to the subjects and investigated how they felt on each road. The subjects were shown videos of three roads and asked about their impressions of each road. The videos were all approximately 15 seconds and were shot between 7 p.m. and 8 p.m.

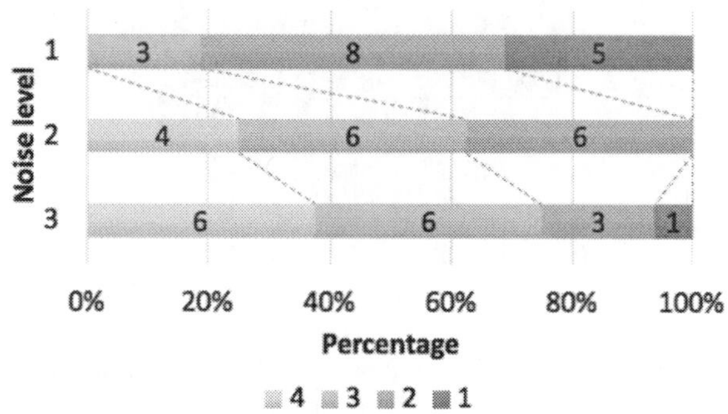

Figure 6. Result of Q.1, "Do you feel fear of crime if you go alone on this road?"

After showing the video to the subject, we asked the subject two questions. Figure 6 is the result of Q. 1, "Do you feel fear of crime if you walk alone on this road?" Answers are given on a four-level Likert scale, in which 4 is "I don't feel afraid" and 1 is "I feel afraid". It can be seen that as the noise level decreases (i.e., the road is estimated to be less busy), more subjects tend to fear crime. Figure 7 is the result of Q. 2, "Do you think you might walk alone on this road at the same time as this video?" Answers are given on a four-level Likert scale, in which 4 is "I think I will pass" and 1 is "I don't think I will pass." It can be seen that the lower the noise level is, the fewer subjects that want to follow the suggested route.

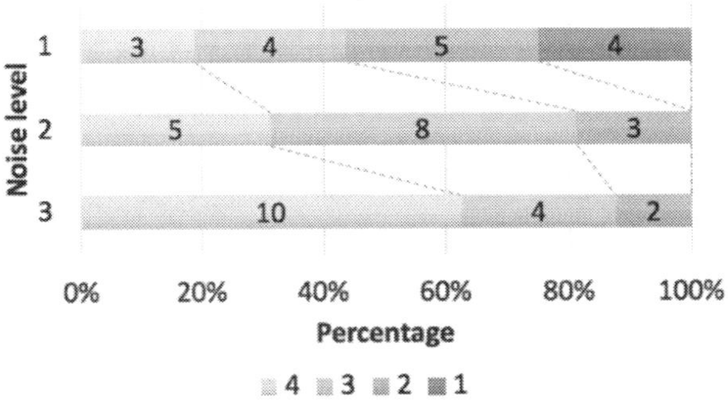

Figure 7. Result of Q.2, "Do you think you might walk alone on this road at the same time as this video?"

From these results, it can be seen that the subjects do not fear crime and do not hesitate to walk on the road that the application has estimated to be the safest (that is, the road where the noise level is high). On the other hand, on the road that the system estimates to be less safe, the subject tends to feel afraid of crime and want to avoid the road. From this result, it can be said that the degree of security estimated by this application is close to the user's feelings. This means that the purpose of this experiment has been confirmed.

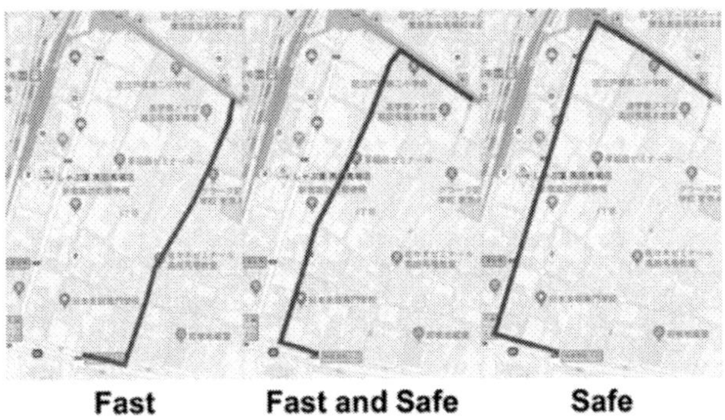

Figure 8. The three routes suggested by our proposed application

C. *Experiment 2-2*

The purpose of this experiment is to make sure that the secure route proposed by the proposed application is beneficial to the user. Three routes searched by the application were presented to the subjects, and we investigated which route was selected. The three routes are a fast route, a fast and safe route, and a safe route. The three routes are shown in Figure 8.

We presented the scenario to each subject before starting the experiment. We examined which route each subject took when he/she was placed in the scenario situation. The scenario is as follows.

D. *Scenario*

You are working at a university doing research. Today is a weekday, and the current time is 7 p.m. After growing tired of working at the university, you decide to move to a coffee shop in Takadanobaba. Because you are worried about walking alone on the road at night, you search for a route you can walk with confidence for your safety using a map-based pedestrian navigation application.

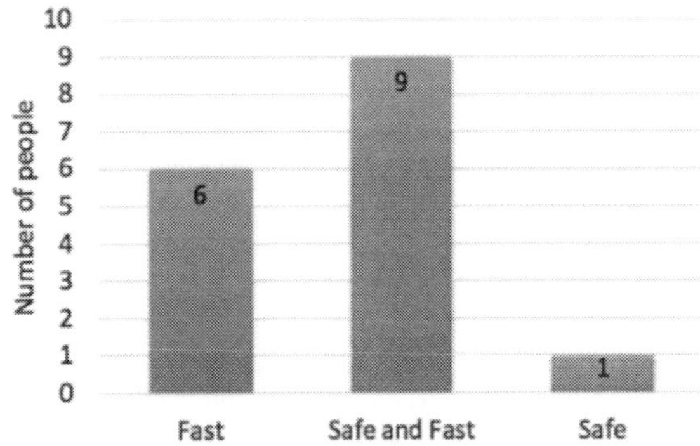

Figure 9. Result of Experiment 2-2

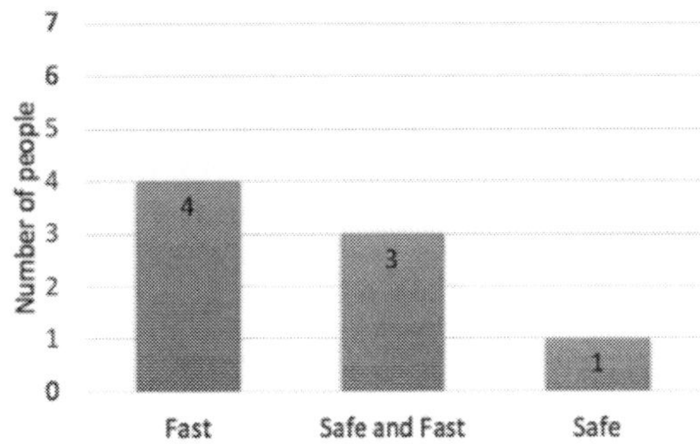

Figure 10. Result of Experiment 2-2 (male)

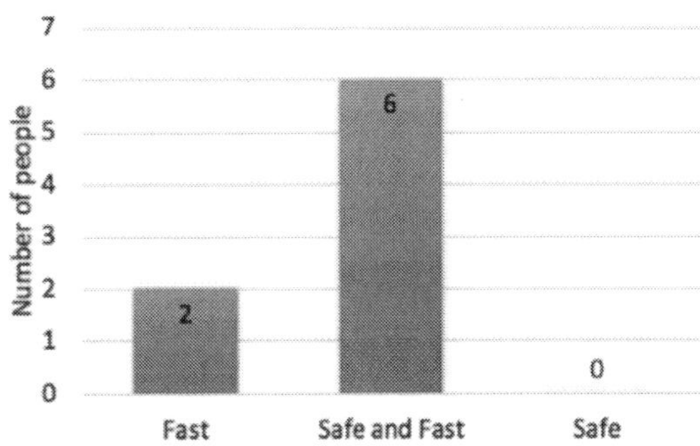

Figure 11. . Result of Experiment 2-2 (female)

E. *Results and Considerations*

The results of the experiment are shown in Figure 9. Ten people chose a fast and safe route or a safe route. This means that 10 people chose route options that are unique to this application. In addition, we asked subjects who chose the shortest route whether they would choose a different route if they were in a city with which they were not familiar or in a foreign country. Five subjects (out of 6) chose routes unique to this application depending on the situation. Thus, the application's unique routes are valuable for 15 out of 16 subjects. This means that the purpose of this experiment has been confirmed.

The results by gender are shown in Figure 10 and Figure 11. The application's unique routes were chosen by 4 of the males and 6 of the females. This finding indicates that the functionality of this map application is more valuable for females than for males.

VI. Conclusion

Through this research, we were able to show that a map-based pedestrian navigation application that presents a safe route is valuable. The application that we created changed the way a certain number of users evaluated routes and reduced fear of crime. It was also verified that noise level data can be used as a criterion for judging safe routes.

In the future, it is necessary to confirm that this application would be of value to many people. In Experiment 2, we investigated the usefulness of our application, but all subjects were in their 20s. It is necessary to determine what kind of result is produced for people from other generations. We should also evaluate the relationship between traffic and noise in different cities. In this study, only the Tokyo city was investigated, but it is necessary to confirm whether the relationship between the traffic and the noise exists in other cities.

We can also think of using a threshold on noisiness. With the route searching algorithm suggested in this paper, very quiet and dark street can be accepted. However, it is not desirable. By using threshold on noisiness, we will be able to avoid suggesting quiet and dark route completely.

We also have to consider a new way to create a data set for noise information. In Experiment 2, we created a data set manually, but in the future, we can easily collect a data and create a data set by using crowdsourcing. This will help us to easily introduce the proposed system to other cities.

References

[1] D. Quercia, R. Schifanella, and L. Maria Aiello, "The shortest path to happiness: recommending beautiful, quiet, and happy routes in the city," HT '14 Proceedings of the 25th ACM conference on Hypertext and social media, pp.116-125, 2014

[2] S. Shah, F. Bao, C.-T. Lu, and I-R. Chen, "CROWDSAFE: crowd sourcing of crime incidents and safe routing on mobile devices," GIS '11 Proceedings of the 19th ACM SIGSPATIAL International Conference on Advances in Geographic Information Systems, pp.521-524, 2011

[3] R. Ohno and Mi. Kondo, "The amount of visual radiation and the sense of safety from crime, A study of the site planning of multi-family housing considering the residents' mutual visual interactions (Part 1)," Journal of Environment Engineering (Transactions of AIJ), No.467, pp.145-151, 1995

[4] K. F. Ferraro and R. L. Grange, "The measurement of fear of crime, Sociological Inquiry," Volume 57, Issue 1, pp.70-97, 1987

[5] M. M. Braungart, R. G. Braungart, and W. J., Hoyer, "Age, Sex, and Social Factors in Fear of Crime, Sociological Focus," Volume 13, No. 1, pp.55-66, 1980

[6] A. K. Brown and M. A. Sturza, "GPS tracking system," United States Patent, 1995

[7] S. van der Spek, J. van Schaick, P. de Bois, and R. de Haan, "Sensing Human Activity: GPS Tracking," Sensors 2009, 9, pp.3033-3055, 2009

[8] H. Chao and R. Gupta, "Image and Video based pedestrian traffic estimation," United States Patent Application Publication, 2013

[9] A. N. Marana, S. A. Velastin, L. F. Costa, and R. A. Lotufo, "Automatic estimation of crowd density using texture," Safety Science, Volume 28, Issue 3, pp.165-175, 1998

[10] R. Watson and P. Yip, "How many were there when it mattered? Estimating the sizes of crowds," Royal Statistical Society, 2011

[11] D. Ryan, S. Denman, S. Sridharan, and C. Fookes, "Scene Invariant Crowd Counting", Digital Image Computing, 2011

[12] E. Kanjo, "NoiseSPY: A Real-Time Mobile Phone Platform for Urban Noise Monitoring and Mapping," Mobile Networks and Applications; New York Volume 15, Issue 4, pp.562-574, 2009

[13] Sound Meter. [Online]. Available from: https://apps.apple.com/jp/app/sound meter / id1093419762 2019.12.25

Optimizing QoE and Cost in a 3D Immersive Media Platform: A Reinforcement Learning Approach

Panagiotis Athanasoulis*, Emmanouil Christakis†, Konstantinos Konstantoudakis†, Petros Drakoulis†, Stamatia Rizou*, Avi Weit‡, Alexandros Doumanoglou†, Nikolaos Zioulis† and Dimitrios Zarpalas†

*Singular Logic S.A., Athens, Greece, Email: pathanasoulis@ep.singularlogic.eu, srizou@singularlogic.eu

†Visual Computing Lab (VCL), Information Technologies Institute (ITI), Centre for Research and Technology - Hellas (CERTH), Thessaloniki, Greece
Email: {manchr, k.konstantoudakis, petros.drakoulis, aldoum, nzioulis, zarpalas}@iti.gr

‡IBM Research, Haifa, Israel, Email: weit@il.ibm.com

***Abstract*—Recent advances in media-related technologies, including capturing and processing, have facilitated novel forms of 3D media content, increasing the degree of user immersion. In order to ensure these technologies can readily support the rising demand for more captivating entertainment, both the production and delivery mechanisms should be transformed to support the application of media or network-related optimizations and refinements on-the-fly. Network peculiarities deriving from geographic and other factors make it difficult for a greedy or a supervised machine learning algorithm to successfully foresee the need for reconfiguration of the content production or delivery procedures. For these reasons, Reinforcement Learning (RL) approaches have lately gained popularity as partial information on the environment is enough for an algorithm to begin its training and converge to an optimal policy. The contribution of this work is a Cognitive Network Optimizer (CNO) in the form of an RL agent, designed to perform corrective actions on both the production and consumption ends of an immersive 3D media platform, depending on a collection of real-time monitoring parameters, including infrastructure, application-level and quality of experience (QoE) metrics. Our work demonstrates CNO approaches with different foci, i.e., a greedy maximization of the users' QoE, a QoE-focused RL approach and a combined QoE-and-Cost RL approach.**

***Index Terms*—immersive media; cognitive network optimizer; reinforcement learning.**

I. Introduction

New forms of interactive 3D media applications have lately emerged as a result of advances in processing, 3D capturing and imaging technologies. These applications include mixed reality and tele-immersive platforms that allow the embedding of real world entities into the virtual world in a real time and interactive way, thus creating a more engaging user experience.

Media applications are justifiably known as some of the most demanding and computationally intensive services, imposing tough challenges on allocation and management procedures, concerning both computing and network resources. State-of-the-art forms of 3D media, ranging from virtual worlds to games, necessitate the rethinking of media production and distribution [1], with the user's Quality-of-Experience (QoE) playing an increasingly dominant role due to the increased level of user immersion. At the same time, it comes as no surprise that the production and delivery costs are rising in order to cater for these novel forms of 3D media content. Ergo, the composition of a real-time, QoE-and-Cost unified, optimization approach is considered essential for these services to remain both affordable and enjoyable. On this ground, recent advancements in the 5G field could provide such enhancements, unleashing the potential of 3D immersive media content, and the media industry in general, through dynamic, real-time refinements and/or reconfiguration of underlying services [2].

In this work, we simulate a 3D-immersive gaming session with all its required components, including simulated consumers of various processing and bandwidth constraints. Our aim is to develop a Cognitive Network Optimizer (CNO) system that manages to balance the consumers' QoE and the quality-transcoding costs. The most common approach would be to either design the CNO in a greedy manner, leveraging statistical knowledge of the overall performance of our targeted system, or apply a machine learning algorithm. Nevertheless, network peculiarities deriving from geographic and other factors, render the application of a supervised machine learning algorithm possibly untrustworthy. A supervised model would heavily depend on the diversity of the networking dataset that would be used, hence, the same model might not perform adequately well across all ranges of network characteristics. On this ground, a Reinforcement Learning (RL) approach was adopted for the design of the aforementioned CNO system, as this kinds of algorithms do not necessarily need prior knowledge in order to perform. Once deployed, a RL agent can learn from the environment through trial-and-error, by receiving positive or negative rewards upon its actions. With RL being the backbone of our envisioned CNO system, it would be possible to present a unified approach for this type of interactive application, possibly able to perform reasonably under any network or processing capacity circumstances.

The rest of this paper is organised as follows: Section II presents the related work while Section III provides insights on the overall system architecture. Section IV depicts the approach that was followed for the design and implementation of the CNO along with essential details. Sections V and VI present the experimental setup and the corresponding results respectively. Finally, Section VII concludes this paper.

II. Related Work

The perceived quality for images and videos has been heavily investigated in the literature and standardized by the International Telecommunication Union (ITU) [3]. However, these recommendations do not readily apply in the case of interactive gaming and 3D reconstruction content. Various works have attempted to model gaming QoE [4]–[7]. We chose to adopt the model described in [7] because the metrics required in order to determine the perceived QoE are readily available in our platform. Although this work examines gaming in its traditional video form, rather than 3D media content, we decided to ignore this discrepancy for two reasons. Firstly, the literature for 3D media quality assessment is still very limited [8]–[10]. It is widely acceptable that formulating a comprehensive QoE model for this kind of media is quite a challenging task. Secondly, the main focus of our work is to demonstrate the capabilities of our CNO system to balance the customers' QoE and the cost of the production platform. This implies that, in principal, any legitimate QoE model could be adopted by our system, thus it is not our focus.

A substantial amount of work has been conducted on adaptive video streaming. The most established technique for this task is MPEG-Dynamic Adaptive Streaming over HTTP (MPEG-DASH) [11]. Recent works have exploited RL to train systems that can accomplish adaptation and have been able to surpass traditional methods in terms of users' QoE [12]–[15], yet, these efforts have solely focused on maximizing the client's satisfaction and have not attempted to balance other factors like the cost of production, which is of great importance for video service providers. Most closely related to our work are [16] and [17], both of which aim to find a balance between cost and QoE. However, contrary to them, we utilize RL to optimize our system, and the content on which our optimizations are performed is 3D reconstructed.

III. System Architecture

The envisioned use-case incorporates a tele-immersive interactive multiplayer video game named "Space Wars", which is developed by [18]. In this application, two players physical appearance is embedded inside a common virtual environment where they interact with each other to play a capture-the-flag style VR game. Players silhouette and texture coverage is being captured using a set of four color-depth (RGB-D) cameras per player, arranged in a square around them. In addition to the players, the system can also accommodate a potentially large number of remotely allocated live spectators, which can be arbitrarily distributed across a wide geographic area. This pushes further the envelope of the underlying infrastructure to include the need for very high bandwidth and near real-time latency, along with highly reliable large-scale delivery. Different parties may have different visual quality requirements, driven by devices capabilities, network conditions or subscription privileges. Thus, the production data streams need to be transcoded into various quality levels in real-time speed, and be concurrently available for consumption in an Adaptive-Bit-Rate (ABR) manner [19].

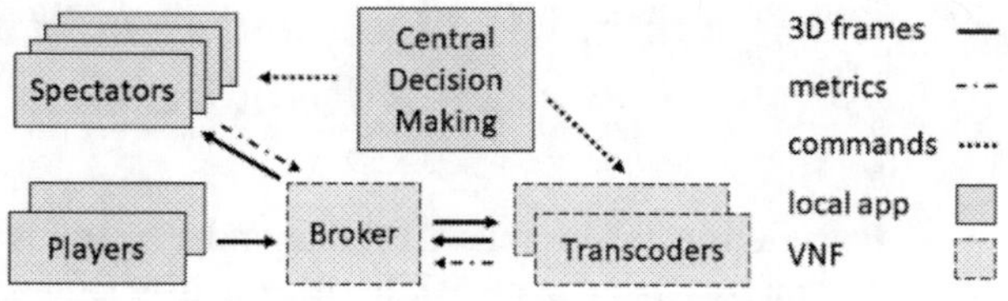

Figure 1. The flow of 3D video frames from the players to the spectators, along with the central decision commands and the metrics that drive them.

In contrast to a typical 3D content delivery pipeline, the examined prototype utilizes many of the forthcoming 5G mannerisms to mitigate the conflicting nature of certain requirements in a resource-efficient, business-friendly way. The opted architecture steps on the model described in [20], where transcoding components are built as Virtual Networking Functions (VNF) and deployed on the 5G-compliant cloud-computing infrastructure (NFVI) opportunistically, in a quality / cost optimized manner. Optimizations may apply in both infrastructure and software level, with only the latter being in scope of this work in the form of management of the quality-levels production and distribution. Optimization strategy and all of the decision-making mechanism is embodied in the CNO component, which translates various network and application-level input measurements to parametrization actions that steer virtual topology towards maximizing the global QoE / cost ratio. A schematic representation of the architecture can be found in Figure 1.

IV. Cognitive Network Optimizer

The role of the CNO is to decide about essential optimizations and corrective actions that should be applied upon both the production and consumption ends of the targeted system, i.e, spectators and transcoders. The CNO, implemented as a RL agent, receives a combination of infrastructure, application-level and QoE metrics, and executes a list of optimization actions. This section provides insights on the CNO's design and implementation, including decisions regarding the implemented algorithm, the selected monitoring parameters and the supported actions.

A. Reinforcement Learning: State-space, Modelling & Reward

Reinforcement Learning is a process of learning in which a situation is mapped to an action in order to maximize either a specific numerical or abstract reward. No advice is given to the entity following the learning procedure, the learner, regarding which actions to take. Instead of this, the learner should discover the rewards that yield from the available actions [21]. The foundation behind most RL algorithms is a Markov Decision Process, composed of:

- a finite number of states S;
- a finite number of actions A;
- a transition function $T : S \times S \times A \rightarrow [0, 1]$ assigning a probability distribution over states;
- a reward function $R : S \times A \times S \rightarrow \mathbb{R}$ giving the immediate reward received after each transition.

The goal of a RL algorithm is to learn a mapping from states to actions, or policy, π. The optimal value of an action a taken from state s, denoted by $V^*(s)$, expresses the expected sum of rewards discounted by a factor γ, that an agent would receive when, starting from state s, the agent performs an action a and follows the optimal policy. The aforementioned values are connected through the following equations:

$$Q^*(s,a) = \sum_{\forall s' \in S} T(s,a,s')[R(s,a,s') + \gamma V^*(s')] \quad (1)$$

$$V^*(s) = \max_{a \in A(s)} \sum_{\forall s' \in S} T(s,a,s')[R(s,a,s') + \gamma V^*(s')] \quad (2)$$

$$\pi^*(s) = arg \max_{a \in A(s)} \sum_{\forall s' \in S} T(s,a,s')[R(s,a,s') + \gamma V^*(s')] \quad (3)$$

The optimal values of the states are the solutions of equation (2). Given the optimal values of the states, the optimal policy is then defined as shown in equation (3).

State-space. In order to capture the complexity of the system in detail, a fine-grained segmentation of the state-space would be required, making the RL agent impractical in terms of required computational resources and training time. Instead of this, a more coarse-grained segmentation of the state-space was preferred. Having gained a thorough understanding of the overall system's performance, leveraging statistical characteristics, and having captured the full value range of the selected monitoring parameters, levels were statically defined for each of these parameters, thus forming a compact, computational resource and training time efficient, state-space.

Modelling Approach. The optimal policy can be calculated following either a model-based or a model-free approach. The model-free approach focuses on the effectiveness of the executed actions, with Q-learning algorithm [22] being its most common representative, an efficient algorithm in terms of required computational and memory resources. Nevertheless, Q-learning performs only local updates to the values, hence only the policy of the initial state can be updated at each step and a large amount of experiences is required to converge to an optimal policy. In the model-based approach, the RL agent tries to model the exact behavior of the environment, thus this approach with Prioritized Sweeping was preferred. Prioritized Sweeping uses careful bookkeeping to concentrate the computational effort on the most interesting parts of the system [23]. After a transition, its probability estimate is updated along with the transition probabilities of previously observed successors.

Reward Function. The reward function is one of the most vital elements of a RL algorithm. It should be designed carefully as it is capable of either assisting the fast convergence of the algorithm or leading to false optimal policies [24]. In our CNO system, the reward function is composed of five reward components aiming for optimizations on different parts of the system: *a) GPU usage*, positive if the application is deployed on a CPU-only node, due to the substantially low cost of such a node, or a GPU-node is used by the majority of spectators, and negative otherwise, *b) QoE of single spectator*, defined as the percentage of increment or decrement of QoE of a spectator after the execution of a certain action, *c) Combination of QoE & transcoding cost*, positive in case the QoE sum of all spectators is greater than the transcoding cost, or negative otherwise, *d) Monitoring parameters*, depending on the percentage of increment or decrement of selected parameters, namely, a spectator's bit rate and frame rate, following the execution of a certain action, and *e) Number of produced profiles*, which gives a positive reward if the number of produced profiles is reduced and a negative reward if it is increased. Of the aforementioned reward components *(b)* and *(d)* are focused on the experience of a single spectator, while *(a)*, *(c)* and *(e)* are focused on the performance and cost of the overall system. Adjustments of the reward components' weights will force the CNO to focus on specific aspects of the system while performing the necessary optimizations.

B. Monitoring Parameters & Optimization Actions

This subsection presents the monitoring parameters that were selected for collection and input to the CNO, along with the optimization actions that are supported by the infrastructure. For the metrics related to containers running on Kubernetes, Prometheus [25] has been employed and two derived metrics expressing the packet loss of the transmitted and received network packets were exported. Besides the Prometheus-exported metrics, application-level metrics are exported from both the spectators and the transcoder VNFs. Moreover, the Mean Opinion Score (MOS) value is computed based on the frame rate and recorded PSNR as described in [7]. Table I presents a list of all metrics used in the optimization process, along with their origin.

The available actions that are selected and executed by the implemented RL algorithm are summarized in Table II. These actions can command *a)* a spectator to start consuming from a specific produced profile (*set_vtranscoder_client_profile*), *b)* a transcoder to start or end production of specific profiles (*set_vtranscoder_profile*), or *c)* a transcoder to migrate from a CPU-only to a GPU-node, or vice-versa (*set_vtranscoder_processing_unit*). Additionally, it is possible that the CNO will detect no need for optimization (*no_operation*). It should be clear that the CNO makes de-

TABLE I
UTILIZED MONITORING METRICS

Origin of Metric	Metric Description
Prometheus (derived metrics)	Transmitted Network Packet Loss Received Network Packet Loss
Spectator	Bit Rate Bit Rate (Aggregated) Frame Rate Frame Rate (Aggregated) Consumed Profile
vTranscoder	Number of Produced Profiles Output Data Bytes Working Frames per Second Theoretic Load Percentage
QoE	Mean Opinion Score

TABLE II
OPTIMIZATION ACTIONS AND SUPPORTED VALUES

Action	Target	Values
set_vtranscoder_client_profile	Spectator	$[0, 1, 2, 3, 4, 5]$
set_vtranscoder_profile	vTranscoder	$[1, 2, 3, 4, 5]$
set_vtranscoder_processing_unit	vTranscoder	[cpu, gpu]
no_operation	-	-

cisions for an action that must be executed on a spectator, yet it is responsible for executing all the essential prerequisite actions as well.

C. Algorithmic Flow

With a certain level of abstraction, the operation of the CNO is described by the algorithm presented in Figure 2. To begin with, the necessary monitoring metrics, as listed in Table I, are collected and the MOS value is computed. This collection of metrics forms a feature vector and is fed to the algorithm. This vector is unequivocally mapped to a state. The determination of the overall system's current state is followed by the establishment of the corrective actions to be executed. A little while after the optimal action's execution, a new set of monitoring metrics will be collected, a new MOS value will be computed and the newly formed feature vector will once again be mapped to a state. Consequently, the reward is computed according to the pre-action and post-action measurements. The latest experience in the form *(pre_action_measurements, action, post_action_measurements, reward)* is recorded and the model values are updated using Prioritized Sweeping.

```
produced_profiles ← [p0]
GPU_profiles ← [pk, ..., pk+n]
pu ← CPU
initial_metrics ← get_collected_measurements()
while True do
    s ← get_state(initial_metrics)
    a, p ← get_suggested_action(s)
    if p ∈ produced_profiles then
        set_vtranscoder_client_profile(p)
    else
        if p ∈ GPU_profiles and pu = CPU then
            set_vtranscoder_processing_unit(GPU)
            pu ← GPU
        produced_profiles.append(p)
        set_vtranscoder_profiles(produced_profiles)
        set_vtranscoder_client_profile(p)
    produced_profiles ← get_consumed_profiles()
    set_vtranscoder_profiles(produced_profiles)
    if pu = GPU and GPU_not_needed() then
        set_vtranscoder_processing_unit(CPU)
        pu ← CPU
    sleep()
    after_metrics ← get_collected_measurements()
    r ← get_reward(initial_metrics, after_metrics)
    update_model()
    initial_metrics ← after_metrics
```

Figure 2. CNO Algorithm

V. EXPERIMENTAL SETUP

To develop our CNO, we simulate the various components required for a "Space Wars" two-players-with-spectators game scenario. For the players, we used an actual game recording between two people. The 3D models and textures of the players are recorded as two streams, one for each player. The resulting streams contain a number of consecutive frames with each frame consisting of four RGB images of a player captured from different angles and a 3D mesh. During the simulation, these two streams are published on a Kafka broker. Then, two transcoders connect on the same broker and each one receives a different stream to produce the extra qualities required to be consumed by the spectators.

The non-transcoded streams deriving directly from the players, namely "passthrough", are produced using jpeg compression for the textures and Google's Draco compression for the meshes. The transcoders can potentially produce five extra qualities. Two of them use jpeg to compress as still images down-scaled versions of the original textures along with more heavily quantized versions of the original meshes, and can be produced solely using the CPU. Another three profiles utilize the HEVC algorithm to encode textures as video sequences, also together with more pronouncedly quantized versions of the meshes, and deliver much higher compression ratios but can only be produced using GPU infrastructure.

All transcoded streams, together with the "passthrough", are published on the broker. The last piece, spectators, also connect to the broker and receive one of the produced qualities. For our experiments, we simulate the spectators so that we can easily modify their bandwidth and processing capabilities, creating various profiles that correspond to real viewing scenarios. The bandwidth of our spectators is set to three different levels: 20, 40 and 60 Mbps, and they can have two different processing capabilities; one corresponding to a low-end mobile user and one to a high-powered desktop one. The processing power of a spectator determines how fast he can decode the incoming frames and in return the frames-per-second (fps) with which he can watch the game. The spectators publish live metrics (downloading bit-rate, viewing fps) on the broker.

Overall, the CNO system analyzes the spectators' metrics and issues a) a command to the transcoders, dictating which qualities they have to produce and b) a command to each spectator to indicate which quality they must consume from every transcoder. As mentioned before, the aim of the CNO is to balance users' QoE with production cost. The production cost is determined by which and how many qualities a transcoder has to produce, directly affecting the underlying CPU or GPU infrastructure needed. A quality that requires GPU to be produced is much more expensive, as is the case on actual commercial services like the Amazon Web Services (AWS), where the leasing price of nodes equipped with GPUs is up to 15 times higher than of nodes without.

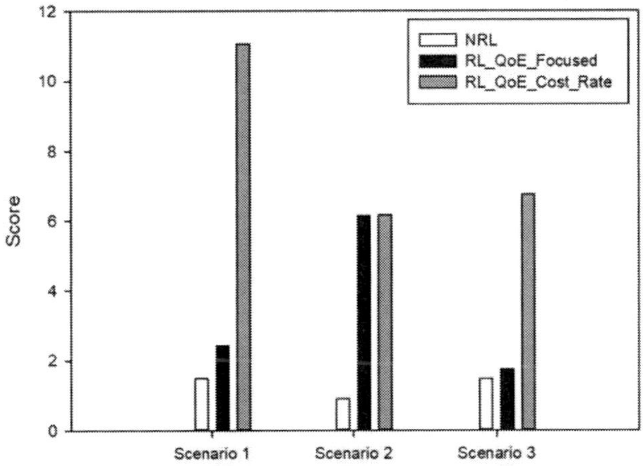

Figure 3. Comparison of the average score achieved at each execution scenario for each CNO configuration

Finally, three CNO versions were examined, namely the *NRL*, implemented as a greedy algorithm targeting on the maximization of the a spectator's QoE, the *RL_QoE_Focused*, implemented as a RL agent with increased weights on its QoE-based reward component, and a combined *RL_QoE_Cost_Rate* version performing joint optimizations between the spectators' QoE and the overall production costs. These CNO versions were executed upon three spectator scenarios. Scenario 1 included spectators of high bandwidth and processing power, Scenario 2 included spectators on the other side of the spectrum, i.e., with low bandwidth and processing power, while Scenario 3 was a mixture of both, also including spectators with moderate bandwidth. For these experiments, we defined the score as the QoE sum of all running spectators divided by the production cost.

VI. Results

This section presents and discusses the results of the executed experiments. Figure 3 offers a performance comparison of each of the CNO configurations, for all three of the different spectator scenarios, while Figures 4a, 4b, and 4c present the progress of score through time, for each scenario. *NRL* receives the lowest average score in all scenarios, while *RL_QoE_Cost_Rate* achieves the highest score. At the same time *RL_QoE_Focused* version is performing well only in Scenario 2, while being marginally better than *NRL* in Scenarios 1 & 3.

The *NRL's* bad performance is due to its sole focus on the maximization of the spectators' QoE, without consideration of the production cost. *NRL* constantly commands the transcoders and spectators to, respectively, produce and consume the most expensive profiles, i.e., profiles that are exclusively produced by GPUs, as these emit the maximum QoE, without considering the higher production costs induced by the GPU's usage, thus reducing its overall score. For this reason, *NRL* achieves its lowest score on Scenario 2, as the GPU's usage makes no difference for these - low bandwidth and processing power - spectators, which cannot keep up with the production under no

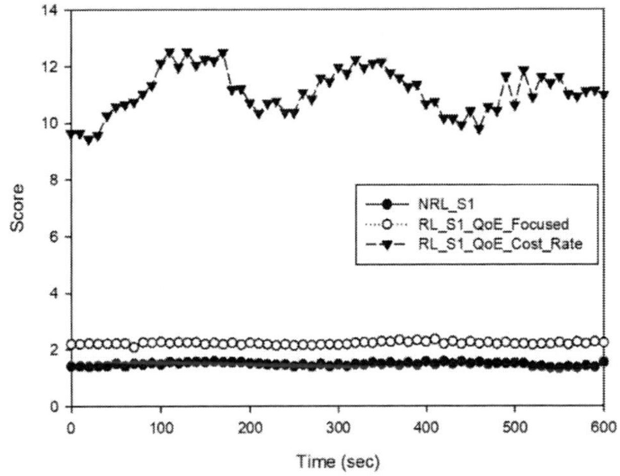

(a) Scenario 1: Spectators with high bandwidth and high processing power

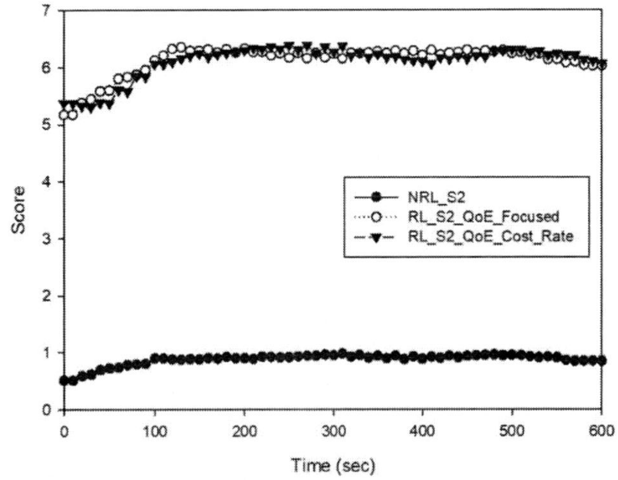

(b) Scenario 2: Spectators with low bandwidth and low processing power

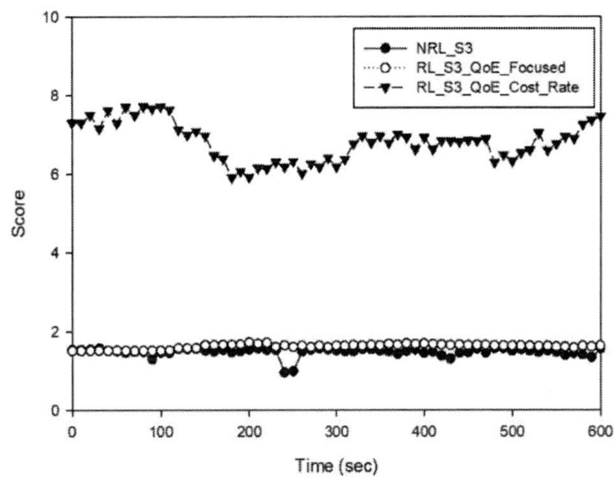

(c) Scenario 3: Combination of bandwidth levels and processing power

Figure 4. Observation of score through time

circumstances. Since these spectators have limited potentials, the best choice in this scenario would be to consume the low-cost CPU-produced profiles, and stop production of the more expensive ones.

Concerning the *RL_QoE_Focused* version, its performance appears almost as bad as the *NRL's* performance in Scenarios 1 & 3. It is thought that in both of these scenarios, the algorithm's decisions were dominated by the high-bandwidth and processing power spectators. Hence, in Scenario 3, the spectators of far inferior capabilities did not effectively affect the CNO's decisions. This statement is supported by the good performance of this version in Scenario 2. Upon detecting spectators with limited capabilities, the algorithm commanded that one of the low-cost CPU profiles should be consumed, thus reducing the overall production cost and increasing score.

Finally, *RL_QoE_Cost_Rate*, considering the spectators' QoE and production cost of as two factors of equal importance, is the most balanced approach and achieves the highest overall score in all scenarios, as originally expected.

VII. Conclusion

The contribution of this work is the implementation and study on the performance of a CNO, implemented as a RL agent aiming for the joint optimization of users' QoE with respect to the production costs. The suggested CNO's operation was validated upon a 3D media platform, in the form of a tele-immersive interactive multiplayer video game with live spectators, adopting many of the forthcoming 5G mannerisms such as supporting dynamic network refinements and reconfiguration in real-time. Three optimization algorithms were examined, a greedy QoE-focused algorithm, a RL algorithm prioritizing the QoE maximization and a combined QoE-and-Cost RL approach. The latter one proved superior in all executed scenarios, in terms of users' QoE / production cost maximization, with QoE-focused RL version being marginally better than the non-RL greedy implementation as well.

Acknowledgment

This research has been partially supported by the European Commission funded program 5G-Media under H2020 Grant Agreement 761699.

References

[1] P. Daras and F. Alvarez, "A future perspective on the 3d media internet." in *Future Internet assembly*, 2009, pp. 303–312.

[2] S. Rizou *et al.*, "A service platform architecture enabling programmable edge-to-cloud virtualization for the 5g media industry," in *2018 IEEE International Symposium on Broadband Multimedia Systems and Broadcasting (BMSB)*. IEEE, 2018, pp. 1–6.

[3] T. ITU, "Opinion model for video-telephony applications," *ITU-T Recommendation P. 1070*, 2007.

[4] I. Slivar, M. Suznjevic, and L. Skorin-Kapov, "The impact of video encoding parameters and game type on qoe for cloud gaming: A case study using the steam platform," in *2015 Seventh International Workshop on Quality of Multimedia Experience (QoMEX)*, May 2015, pp. 1–6.

[5] I. Slivar, L. Skorin-Kapov, and M. Suznjevic, "Cloud gaming qoe models for deriving video encoding adaptation strategies," in *Proceedings of the 7th International Conference on Multimedia Systems*, ser. MMSys '16. New York, NY, USA: ACM, 2016, pp. 18:1–18:12. [Online]. Available: http://doi.acm.org/10.1145/2910017.2910602

[6] S. Wang and S. Dey, "Modeling and characterizing user experience in a cloud server based mobile gaming approach," in *GLOBECOM 2009 - 2009 IEEE Global Telecommunications Conference*, Nov 2009, pp. 1–7.

[7] S. Zadtootaghaj, S. Schmidt, and S. Mller, "Modeling gaming qoe: Towards the impact of frame rate and bit rate on cloud gaming," in *2018 Tenth International Conference on Quality of Multimedia Experience (QoMEX)*, May 2018, pp. 1–6.

[8] A. Doumanoglou, N. Zioulis, E. Christakis, D. Zarpalas, and P. Daras, "Subjective quality assessment of textured human full-body 3d-reconstructions," in *2018 Tenth International Conference on Quality of Multimedia Experience (QoMEX)*, May 2018, pp. 1–6.

[9] A. Doumanoglou *et al.*, "Quality of experience for 3-d immersive media streaming," *IEEE Transactions on Broadcasting*, vol. 64, no. 2, pp. 379–391, June 2018.

[10] E. Alexiou and T. Ebrahimi, "On subjective and objective quality evaluation of point cloud geometry," in *2017 Ninth International Conference on Quality of Multimedia Experience (QoMEX)*, May 2017, pp. 1–3.

[11] I. Sodagar, "The mpeg-dash standard for multimedia streaming over the internet," *IEEE MultiMedia*, vol. 18, no. 4, pp. 62–67, April 2011.

[12] H. Mao, R. Netravali, and M. Alizadeh, "Neural adaptive video streaming with pensieve," in *Proceedings of the Conference of the ACM Special Interest Group on Data Communication*, ser. SIGCOMM '17. New York, NY, USA: ACM, 2017, pp. 197–210. [Online]. Available: http://doi.acm.org/10.1145/3098822.3098843

[13] M. Claeys, S. Latr, J. Famaey, and F. De Turck, "Design and evaluation of a self-learning http adaptive video streaming client," *IEEE Communications Letters*, vol. 18, no. 4, pp. 716–719, April 2014.

[14] M. Xing, S. Xiang, and L. Cai, "Rate adaptation strategy for video streaming over multiple wireless access networks," in *2012 IEEE Global Communications Conference (GLOBECOM)*, Dec 2012, pp. 5745–5750.

[15] V. Menkovski and A. Liotta, "Intelligent control for adaptive video streaming," in *2013 IEEE International Conference on Consumer Electronics (ICCE)*, Jan 2013, pp. 127–128.

[16] J. He, Y. Wen, J. Huang, and D. Wu, "On the costqoe tradeoff for cloud-based video streaming under amazon ec2's pricing models," *IEEE Transactions on Circuits and Systems for Video Technology*, vol. 24, no. 4, pp. 669–680, April 2014.

[17] Y. Zheng *et al.*, "Online cloud transcoding and distribution for crowdsourced live game video streaming," *IEEE Transactions on Circuits and Systems for Video Technology*, vol. 27, no. 8, pp. 1777–1789, Aug 2017.

[18] K. Christaki, K. Apostolakis, A. Doumanoglou, N. Zioulis, D. Zarpalas, and P. Daras, "Space wars: An augmentedvr game," 2018.

[19] J. Kua, G. Armitage, and P. Branch, "A survey of rate adaptation techniques for dynamic adaptive streaming over http," *IEEE Communications Surveys Tutorials*, vol. 19, pp. 1842–1866, 2017.

[20] A. Doumanoglou *et al.*, "A system architecture for live immersive 3d-media transcoding over 5g networks," in *2018 IEEE International Symposium on Broadband Multimedia Systems and Broadcasting (BMSB)*. IEEE, 2018, pp. 11–15.

[21] R. S. Sutton and A. G. Barto, *Reinforcement learning: An introduction*. MIT press, 2018.

[22] C. J. Watkins and P. Dayan, "Q-learning," *Machine learning*, vol. 8, no. 3-4, pp. 279–292, 1992.

[23] A. W. Moore and C. G. Atkeson, "Prioritized sweeping: Reinforcement learning with less data and less time," *Machine learning*, vol. 13, no. 1, pp. 103–130, 1993.

[24] L. Matignon, G. J. Laurent, and N. Le Fort-Piat, "Reward function and initial values: better choices for accelerated goal-directed reinforcement learning," in *International Conference on Artificial Neural Networks*. Springer, 2006, pp. 840–849.

[25] Prometheus monitoring system & time series database. [Online]. Available: https://prometheus.io/

Embedding Information in 3D Printed Objects with Curved Surfaces Using Near Infrared Fluorescent Dye

*Piyarat Silapasuphakornwong, **Hideyuki Torii,
**Kazutake Uehira
Human Media Research Center
Kanagawa Institute of Technology
Atsugi, Japan
*e-mail: silpiyarat@gmail.com,
**email: {torii, uehira}@nw.kanagawa-it.ac.jp

Siravich Chandenduang
Department of Mathematic & Computer Science
Chulalongkorn University
Bangkok, Thailand
e-mail: Siravich93@gmail.com

Abstract—**This paper presents a technique to embed barcodes in the curved surfaces of objects fabricated with a 3D printer. The objects are fabricated using resin material, and the barcodes patterns inside an object are formed using the same resin material as other regions but containing a small amount of fluorescent dye. When these objects are irradiated with near-infrared rays, fluorescent dyes are excited, and they emit near-infrared fluorescence. Therefore, the internal barcode patterns can be captured as high-contrast images using a near-infrared camera, and the information expressed by the barcodes inside the objects can be nondestructively read out. We conducted experiments to demonstrate that this technique can also be applied to objects with curved surfaces. A sample was prepared using a 3D printer with two-head fused deposition modeling. The experimental results show that we can hide a barcode inside an object so that no one can see it from the outside and that we can decode all barcodes correctly with 100% accuracy.**

Keywords-3D printer; information hiding; near infrared light; fluorescent dye.

I. Introduction

3D printers have been attracting attention as a new method of manufacturing. This is because consumers can easily obtain a product that they want just by buying the model data through the Internet and print it if they have a 3D printer in their own home or office. 3D printers have been reduced in price and miniaturized. Notice that we could not see the barcodes from outside all of the sample. Thus, the barcodes were hidden completely. Thus, 3D printers are expected to revolutionize distribution and manufacturing in the future [1] – [3].

3D printers use a unique process called additive manufacturing in which thin layers are formed one by one to create an object [4]. This enables forming any structure inside the object. We have used this feature in our study on the techniques of embedding information inside a 3D printed object, and we were able to form fine patterns inside the object to express information [5] – [9].

The embedding of information inside 3D printed objects will enable adding extra value to these objects. For example, we can embed information that usually comes with newly purchased products into them. Moreover, it will be possible to use them as "things" of the Internet of Things (IoT) in connecting to the Internet.

We have studied some methods of forming fine patterns inside a 3D printed object that used a Fused Deposition Modeling (FDM) 3D printer with resin as a material. One of them is a method that forms internal patterns using resin containing a small amount of fluorescent dye [10]. Fluorescent dye emits fluorescence when near-infrared rays are irradiated; therefore, the internal pattern can be captured as a high-contrast image using a near-infrared camera. This enhances the readability of the embedded information.

So far, we have demonstrated the feasibility of this technique and also the possibility of high density information embedding by forming inside patterns at double depth [11]. This study was conducted using flat surface sample objects because they were intended to determine the feasibility and because flat surfaces made the experiment easy. However, we have to demonstrate that this technique can also be applied to many general objects for practical use because such objects usually have curved surfaces. This paper describes our experiments using objects with curved surfaces and the results we obtained.

The rest of the paper is organized as follows: the principle of basic embedding fluorescent dye into a fabricate object and its readout method are described in Section II. Then, we show the feasibility and method how to embedding barcodes under the curve surface and evaluation in Section III. Next, Section IV is the results and discussions, followed by the conclusion in Section V, respectively.

II. Information Embedding Using Fluorescent Dye

The technique of using fluorescent dye for internal patterns is illustrated by Figure 1. This technique assumes that the resin is used as an object material. Pattern regions inside the object are formed using the same resin as that of other regions, but they contain a small amount of fluorescent dye. Because resin has high transmittance for near infrared, the rays reach the internal fluorescent dyes when the object is irradiated with near-infrared rays from the outside. The light source irradiates light with wavelength λ_E, which excites the fluorescent dye. The fluorescent dye is then excited and emits fluorescence. Therefore, a bright image of the patterns inside the resin object can be captured.

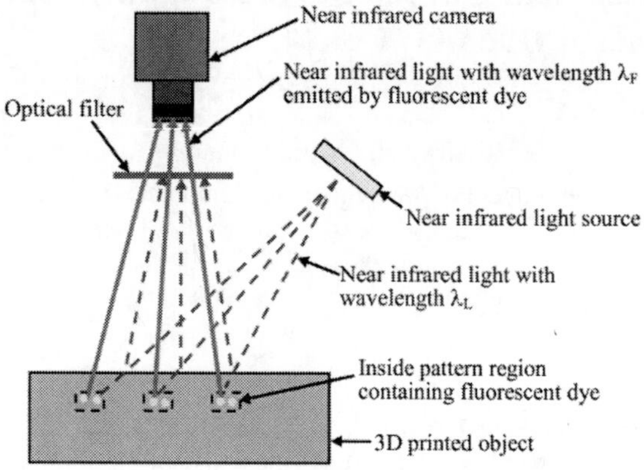

Figure 1. Basic concept of proposed technique [10]

Because wavelength λ_F of the dye's fluorescence differs from wavelength λ_E of the irradiated light, only light the fluorescent dye emits enters the camera using an optical filter that blocks the light from the source. In our previous studies where near infrared rays were used, reflective light from the object surface also entered the camera as noise. This decreased the readability of the embedded information. In contrast, because the technique in this study can block such reflective light from the surface, a low noise image of the pattern should be obtainable, enhancing readability.

The patterns cannot be seen with the naked eye from the outside using the same color of resins for the body and internal patterns even if they are formed in a very shallow position from the surface. This is because the amount of the fluorescent dye contained in the resin is very small, and this hardly changes the color. This is important for applications requiring embedded information to remain hidden.

III. EXPERIMENTS

In this paper, we focus on applying this technique to the curved objects in order to confirm the feasibility to apply in practical general 3D objects. Most general 3D objects have curved surfaces. The difference in the incidence and reflection of light on the curved surface is irregular. It may have some effects on the appearance in captured images, such as brightness and contrast. Therefore, it could affect the readability of the read-out process in the end. Hence, we set up experiments to find the appropriate factors in our technique concerning when our technique should be applied in practical situations.

A. *Sample preparation*

We prepared samples and evaluated the results using the workflow shown in Figure 2. The 3D models were built from a CAD program. With this step, barcodes containing information on the word "Hi" were embedded and hidden inside the 3D models, as shown in Figure 3. We varied the depth of embedding the barcodes at 0.5 and 1.0 mm, and we placed them in 3D models such as a half sphere and a half cylinder to compare the effect of the curved surfaces on the samples. The space between each line of the barcodes was at

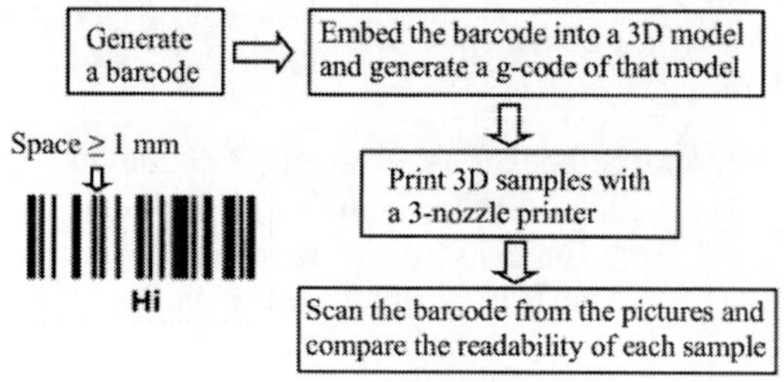

Figure 2. Workflow of experiment

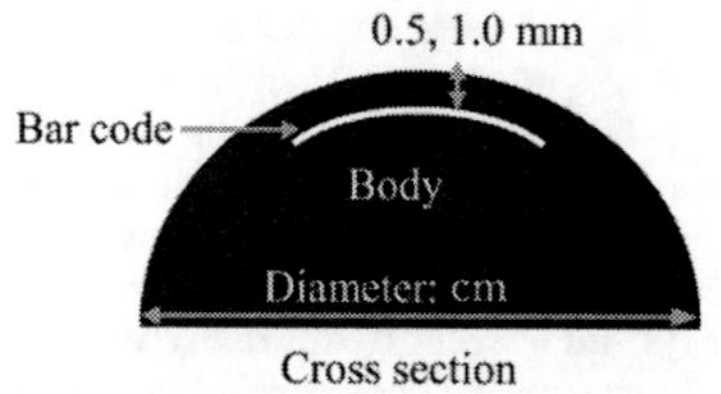

Figure 3. Cross section of our sample used in the experiment

TABLE I. DESIGNED SAMPLES IN EXPERIMENTS

3D Model	Diameter (cm)	Depth of barcode from surface (mm)
Sphere	8	0.5
		1.0
Cylinder	4.5	0.5
		1.0

least 1 mm, and the size of each line was 1 mm. The design of the samples is shown in Table I. Then, a sample file was generated in the g-code file for slicing. After that, the samples were created using a 3D printer with two nozzles, one nozzle being a normal ABS and the other being an ABS-fluorescent dye mixed filament, as shown in Figure 4 (left). After printing, we captured images of samples using a near infrared camera with a specific optical filter. The barcodes, which were embedded inside the objects, would then appear. Finally, we scanned the barcodes of the pictures we took and compared the readability of each object.

B. *Capture of near infrared images*

We used a near infrared CCD camera with a specific optical filter to capture the images of the hidden barcodes inside the samples. The resolution of the images was 2048 x 1088 pixels. The layout of the samples with instruments is shown in Figure 4 (right). To read out the data embedded in the objects, we used a QR & barcode scanner application available on Android and a QR-scanner application available on iOS for decoding the barcodes. However, some images could not be read out directly from the capturing process. To solve this problem, we enhanced them by adjusting their sharpness using the sharpness enhancement mode provided by Microsoft PowerPoint. Then, we repeated the scanning

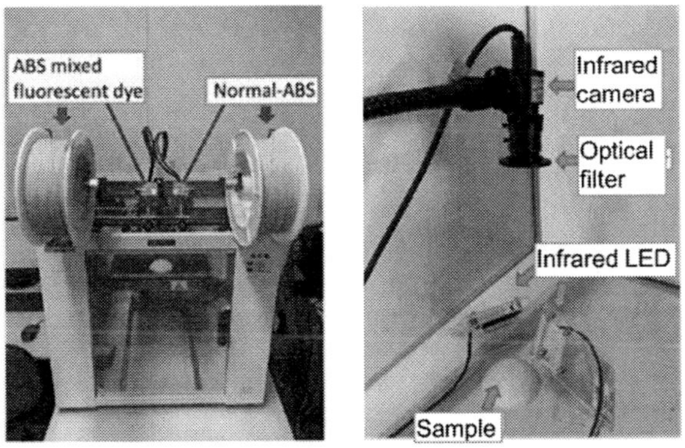

Figure 4. Experiment setup: (left) a two-nozzle printer, (right) Layout of instruments for evaluation

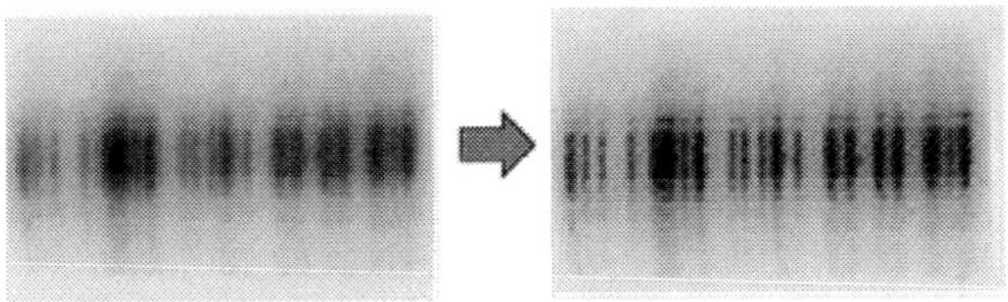

Figure 5. Enhancement process: (left) before enhancement, (right) after enhancement by adjusting sharpness

step. The enhancement process is shown in Figure 5.

We tried to read out the barcodes using the automatic barcode scanner application ten times and reported the % accuracy, both in before and after enhancement images, as determined with the following equation. The accuracy measures how it is easy to access to readout barcodes—change to word or some understandable information.

$$\% \text{ accuracy} = \frac{times\ of\ readout\ success}{Total\ numbers\ of\ readout} \quad (1)$$

IV. Results and Discussion

Table II shows the 3D models of the half spheres and cylinders after printing them with the bar code depth varied at 0.5 and 1.0 mm below the surface and the readout results, respectively. Notice that we could not see the barcodes from outside all of the samples. Thus, the barcodes were hidden completely.

When the depth of 0.5 mm was used in both the half sphere and cylinder surfaces, the barcodes could be read out within a second (almost immediately), and no sharpness enhancement was needed. We could decode from the captured images directly.

Nevertheless, for an embedding depth of 1.0 mm, both the half sphere and cylinder surfaces could be read out using the same application, but more time was needed, along with an ideal position to read the barcodes. Thus, the sharpness needed to be improved. After sharpness was enhanced, they could be read out within a second (almost immediately). Also, the results of the embedding depth of 0.5 mm were the same.

The samples of the embedding depth barcode of 1.0 mm could not be read out directly because of the irregularity of incident and reflect lighting on the curved surfaces. The curves of the surfaces made the distance different between the barcodes to the light and camera in each area. The center of the curves was the highest. Hence, we could capture the images very clearly because they were near the camera and in the point of focus. However, the barcodes at the curved rims were the farthest from the camera, making the capture images from this area very blurry and unreadable because they were out of focus.

However, after the enhancing process, the barcodes could be read out effectively. We tried to enhance the sharpness of images in both the 0.5 and 1.0 mm samples. The results were that they could be read smoothly. That let us know that the sharpness was an important factor for our technique to ensure the readability of the hidden barcodes inside 3D models. Hence, we will utilize our method to enhance the sharpness of captured barcode images for effective readouts when our technique will be applied in practical applications for embedding information in general 3D models, the main target for our study. That will make the information on decoding more accurate and make the readability more

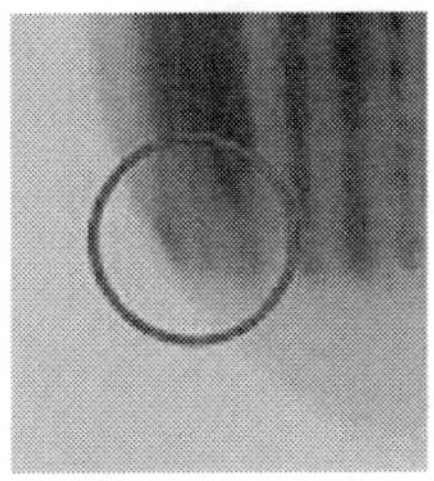

Figure 6. Problem of barcode at the rim of the curved surface model

efficient.

Moreover, we will endeavor to embed QR codes instead of barcodes in future work because they can increase the amount of embedded information, though they will increase the difficulty of readouts. With the principle of reading out the barcodes, the patterns just clarify only a tab where the length is greater than the width at a propagation of 2:1. This will make the barcodes much easier to decode than QR codes. For QR codes, all of their positions have to be completely clear. The rim of the curved surfaces mainly cause a problem with reading because the images are blurry and the codes distort (caused by the shape model and printing), as shown in Figure 6. Thus, we have to determine feasibility in future work for this reason.

V. Conclusion

We proposed a technique of non-destructively reading out information embedded inside curved objects using near-infrared light. We determined the feasibility of applying our technique to general non-flat models by creating 3D curved samples, such as spheres and cylinders, by varying the depth

TABLE II. RESULTS OF EXPERIMENTS

Model: Embedded Depth (mm)	Real Printed Object	Captured Infrared Image	Readability	After Enhancing Image	Readability
Sphere: 0.5 mm	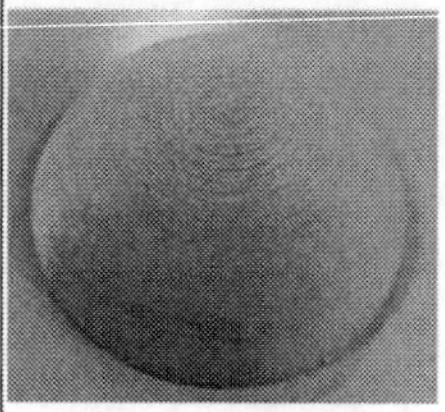	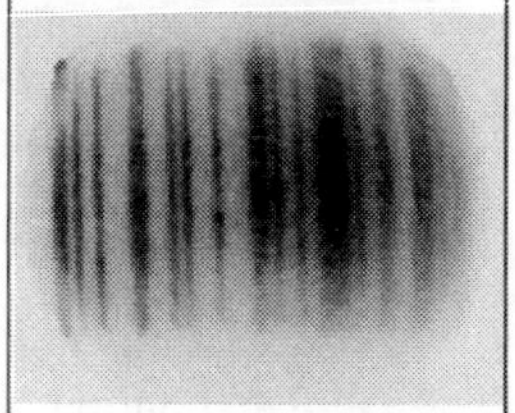	√ (Fast) 100%	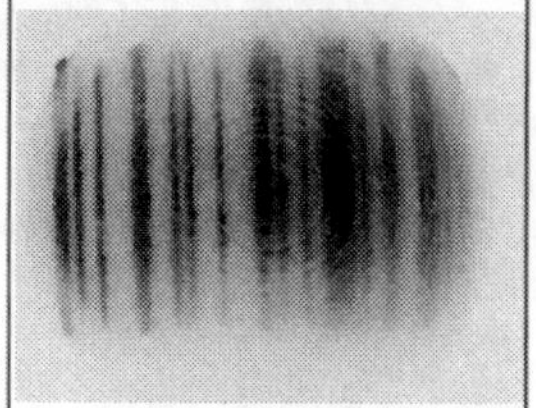	√ (Immediate) 100%
Sphere: 1.0 mm	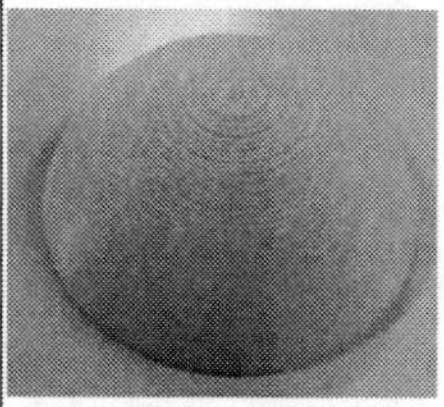	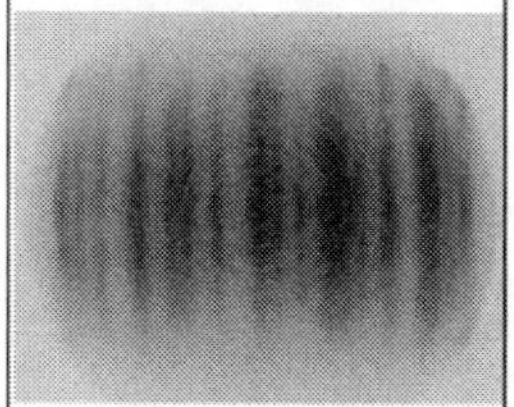	X (Only from an ideal position & with slow readout) 50%	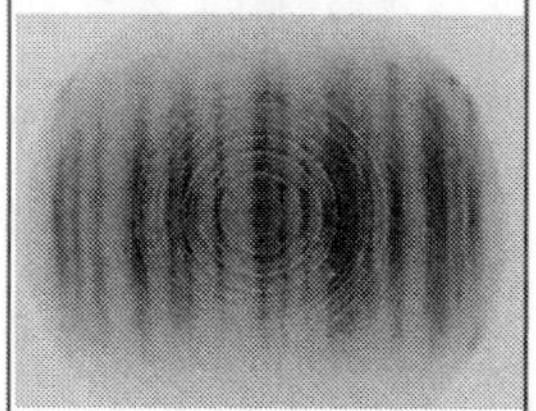	√ (Fast) 100%
Cylinder: 0.5 mm	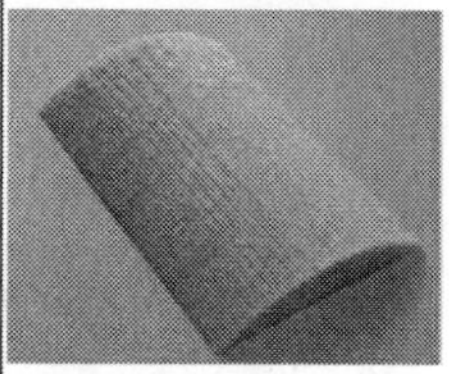	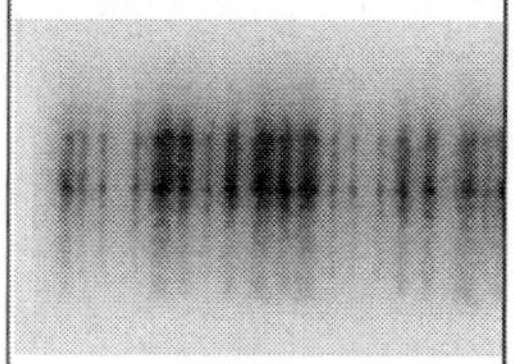	√ (Fast) 100%	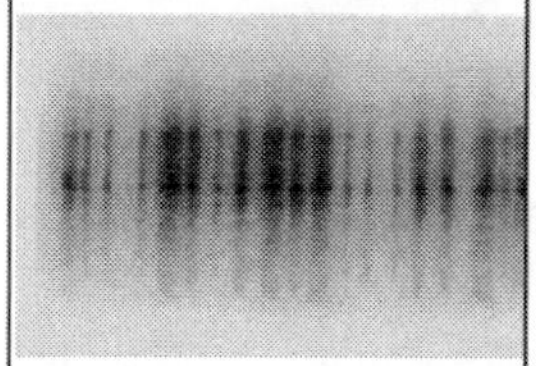	√ (Immediate) 100%
Cylinder: 1.0 mm	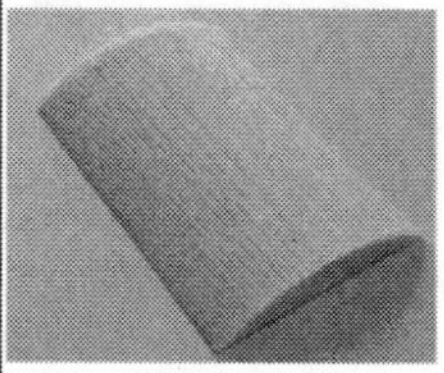	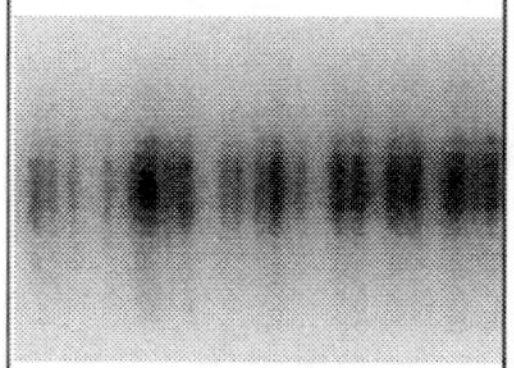	X (Only from an ideal position & with slow readout) 50%	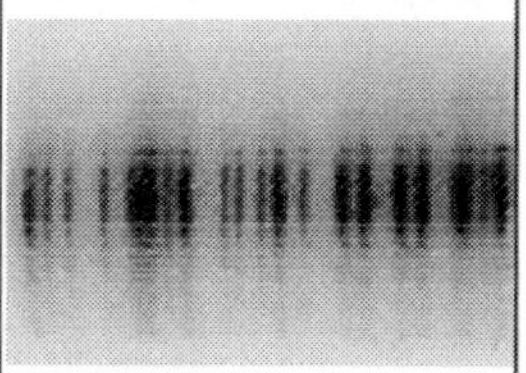	√ (Fast) 100%

below the surface of barcodes between 0.5 and 1.0 mm, and by comparing the same model with different barcode depths. The results showed the feasibility of hiding the barcodes inside the objects so that no one can see even part of them from the outside and the feasibility of decoding all the barcodes correctly with 100% accuracy. The best barcode depth for embedding was found to be 0.5 mm. Although, at the depth of 1.0 mm, we could not read out the barcodes directly from the captured images, enhancing the process helped with reading out the barcodes correctly. We found that sharpness was an importance factor of readability in our technique, for both 0.5 and 1.0 mm surface embedded thickness. We can choose to embed information at a depth of 0.5 mm from the surface in 3D printed objects. At this depth, we do not need any sharpness enhancement to read out information, ensuring the best conditions, convenience, and efficiency for use in practical applications. The target of our study is to apply our proposed method to cover all cases of real-world printed objects in the future. Thus, we will also try to embed QR codes instead of barcodes in both flat, curved, and general surfaces in order to increase the amount of information embedding effectively.

ACKNOWLEDGMENT

We would like to thank DIC Corporation for providing the fluorescent dye contained in the ABS resin in this research.

REFERENCES

[1] B. Berman, "3-D printing: The new industrial revolution," Business horizons, vol. 55, no. 2, pp. 155–162, March–April 2012.

[2] B. Garrett, "3D printing: New economic paradigms and strategic shifts," Global Policy, vol. 5, no. 1, pp. 70–75, February 2014.

[3] C. Weller, R. Kleer, and F. T. Piller, "Economic implications of 3D printing: Market structure models in light of additive manufacturing revisited," International Journal of Production Economics, vol. 164, pp. 43–56, June 2015.

[4] F. Hartung and M. Kutter, "Multimedia watermarking techniques" Proc IEEE, Vol. 87, No. 7, pp. 1079–1107, 1999.

[5] M. Suzuki, P. Silapasuphakornwong, K. Uehira, H. Unno, and Y. Takashima, "Copyright protection for 3D printing by embedding information inside real fabricated objects," International Conference on Computer Vision Theory and Applications, pp. 180–185, March 2015.

[6] M. Suzuki, et al., "Embedding Information into Objects Fabricated With 3-D Printers by Forming Fine Cavities inside Them", Proceedings of IS&T International symposium on Electronic Imaging, Vol. 2017, No. 41, pp. 6–9, 2017 .

[7] P. Silapasuphakornwong, et al., "Nondestructive readout of copyright information embedded in objects fabricated with 3-D printers", The 14th International Workshop on Digital-forensics and Watermarking, Revised Selected Papers, pp. 232–238, 2016.

[8] K. Uehira, et al., "Copyright Protection for 3D Printing by Embedding Information Inside 3D-Printed Objects", The 15th International Workshop on Digital-forensics and Watermarking Revised Selected Papers, pp. 370–378, 2017.

[9] K. D. D. Willis and A. D. Wilson, "Infrastructs: Fabricating Information Inside Physical Objects for Imaging in the Terahertz Region", ACM Transactions on Graphics, Vol. 32, No. 4, pp. 138-1–138-10, July 2013.

[10] P. Silapasuphakornwong, M. Suzuki, H. Torii, and K. Uehira, "Technique for embedding information in objects produced with 3D printer using near infrared fluorescent dye", Proceedings of MMEDIA, pp. 55-58, 2019.

[11] H. Kasuga, P. Silapasuphakornwong, H. Torii, M. Suzuki, and K. Uehira, "Technique to Embed Information in 3D Printed Objects Using Near Infrared Fluorescent Dye", Proceedings of IECIE, 2019.

Seamless Audio Melding: Using Seam Carving with Music Playlists

Michele Covell and Shumeet Baluja
Google Research
Mountain View, California 94043, USA
email: covell@google.com, shumeet@google.com

***Abstract*—In both studio and live performances, professional music DJs in an increasing number of popular musical genres mix recordings together into continuous streams that progress seamlessly from one song to the next. When done well, these create an engaging and seamless experience, as if they were part of a single performance. This work introduces a new way to provide that continuity using not only beat matching, but also frequency-dependent cross fades. The basis of our technique is derived from the well developed technique of visual-seam carving, most commonly found in computer vision and graphics systems. We adapt visual seam carving to indicate the times at which to transition specific frequencies from one song to the next. Additionally, we also describe a way to invert the melded spectrogram with minimal computation. The entire system works faster than real-time to provide the ability to use this system in live performances.**

Keywords–Music; Seam Carving; Tempo Estimation; Beat Matching; Spectrogram Inversion

I. INTRODUCTION

Music is used as a background to many of our daily activities. Minimizing the perception of breaks or sudden changes to the music can ensure that obtrusive start-stop artifacts do not hinder our focus on our principal activity, be it exercising, socializing, dancing, or concentrating on work. In the context of parties and nightclubs, many professional DJs have mastered the art of maintaining the illusion of continuous music, even while moving from one song to another.

The area of song-sequence selection (what order to play songs) is widely researched [1][2], especially now that numerous streaming-music services are available [3][4]. However, most of these services do not smoothly transition from one song to another. They offer "focus mixes", "party mixes", and "workout mixes", where the best user experience would be to have the songs flow into one another, but they keep the tracks clearly separated in playback. Even when automated mixing is provided, if it is not done well, users are likely to avoid the feature [5]. There are software packages for mixing songs (*e.g.*, [6]) but these rely on time-domain beat matching and cross-fading, without regard to the different energy and matching profiles across different frequency ranges. Other prototype systems, such as those in [5][7][8] have tackled the task of consecutive song-melding, using and extending the commonly used beat matching baseline. In particular, [5] calculates specific timbre, chrome, loudness, and "vocalness" features to help select the best transition points.

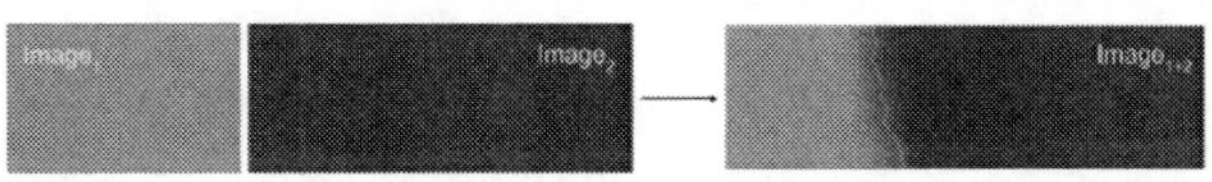

Figure 1: A seam is chosen as the center for the combining of two images after they are registered to each other.

Our work, in contrast to that described above, does not calculate explicit features. Instead, we tackle the song-mixing task by moving to the frequency domain and using techniques from visual scene carving [9]. To redefine this primarily visual tool for use in audio, we begin by using the spectrogram as the fundamental "image" on which operate. A brief description of seam carving is provided next.

Originally, seam carving was developed as a technique for image resizing that takes into account the content of the image but many researchers found a practical use beyond image cropping: image stitching and compositing [10][11][12][13]. When two images (*e.g.*, aerial photographs of the ground) are to be stitched together, the overlapping regions may have blurring or "ghosting" if naively placed on top of each other. To address this, after the images are registered to each other, a seam is found within the overlapping region of the images. As illustrated in Figure 1, the seam is used as the anchor from which the blending is done; the pixels around the seam are weighted and merged together. The best results are achieved when the seams between the two images travel on a path which introduces the *least change* in the local visual structure, as measured by gradient magnitude on the composite result. This seam can be found using straight-forward dynamic programming. See [14] for a particularly good explanation of the process.

The parallels from image stitching to the task of audio melding are clear. Analogously, we are given two songs to "stitch" together. If done poorly, for example with incorrect registration, the equivalent of visual ghosting will occur. We attempt to reduce the amount of such distortions and sonic "muddiness" in the resulting blend by finding a low energy seam within the well-aligned spectrograms of the two songs.

To make the system suitable for practical use, note that even though we operate in the frequency domain, requiring spectrogram inversion, we are able to complete the process in less time than it takes to play the melded songs, due to careful attention to keeping our operations local.

As outlined in Section II (with details in the appendix), our system splits tempo estimation, speed adjustment, and beat alignment from the seam carving itself. Section III then describes our approach to selecting the frequency-dependent start and end of the seam carving on the aligned spectrograms. In Section IV, we introduce improvements to spectrogram inversion [15], allowing us to limit our inversion computation to the time intervals around each song transition, instead of

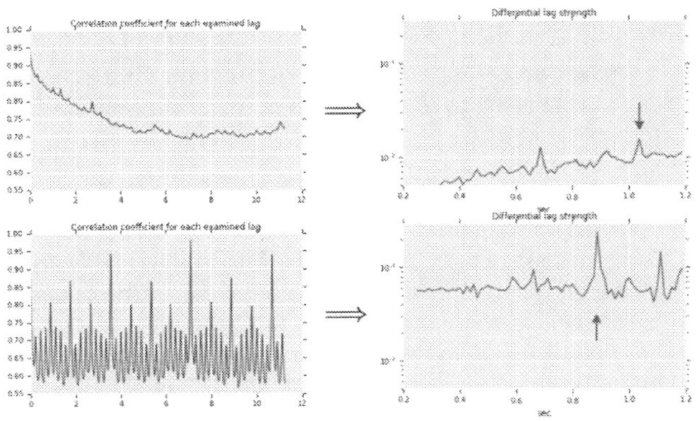

Figure 2: Correlation coefficients, $\rho[l]$ (left), and tempo measure curves, $t[l]$ (right), for segments with a weak (top) and a weak (bottom) beat. (Selected tempos shown with arrows.)

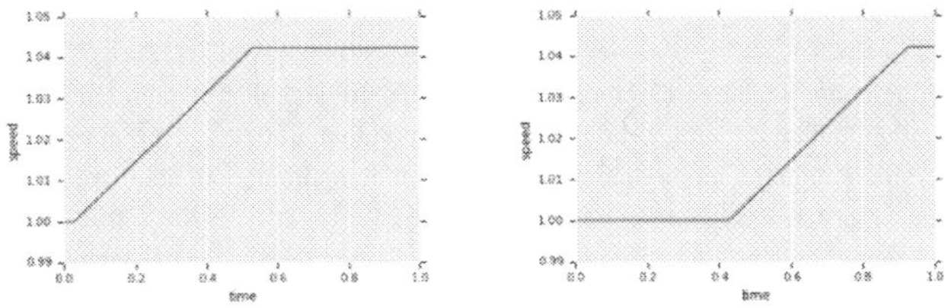

a) (continuing from Figure 2) weak- to strong-tempo speeds

b) strong- to weak-tempo speeds

Figure 3: Example speed profiles for transitions between different-strength tempos.

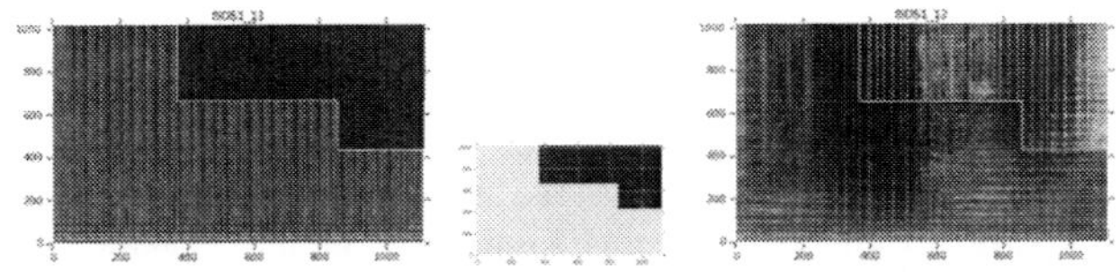

Figure 4: Carving of aligned spectrograms: overlapping aligned spectral sections (left/right) and mask used to meld them (center).

needing to coordinate across the full play list. Finally, Sections V and VI provide results and conclusions, respectively.

II. Pre-processing, Tempo Estimation and Alignment

Many of the existing DJ systems are based on tempo estimation and matching. This is also the first conceptually interesting part of our system. However, for robustness to recording durations, we start by trimming silences from the end of the "current" song (the song that is coming to an end) and from the beginning of the "next" song (the song that is starting). On these silence-trimmed tracks, we then compute the spectrogram for the last/first 40 seconds of the current/next songs. (The detailed parameters for our spectrograms are provided in our appendix.) Going forward, we will refer to these 40-second duration spectrograms from the end of the current songs as the *current segment*, and the 40-second duration spectrograms from the beginning of the next songs as the *next segment*.

We estimate the tempo on both the current/next segments, so that we can match beats during segment alignment. As detailed in the appendix, we use an approach that is somewhat similar to beat histograms [16], using the coherence of the beat's sub-harmonics to clarify which peaks in the auto correlation correspond to stable repetitions. Operating only on the 40-second segments at the end/beginning of the current/next songs, we can determine a list of candidate tempos. Using Figure 2 as an example, the current song (top) has a weak tempo (only 0.016 by our differential-strength measure) which is most prominent at 1.04 sec/beat, but with two weaker alternatives at 0.69 and 0.93 sec/beat, while the next song (bottom) has a very strong tempo (0.25 by our differential-strength measure) which is most prominent at 0.89 sec/beat (and several secondary candidates).

We use our estimated tempos for our current and next segments to resample their spectrograms in a way that the two tempos appear the same, balancing the strength of each candidate pairing with the likely audibility of the speed change that the pairing would require. Continuing with the example from Figure 2, we find our best balance between these factors leads us to use a 4.2% speed-up (pairing the 0.93 and 0.89 sec-per-beat candidates). We (in effect) resample the current/next spectrograms to bring the two tempos into alignment, using a speed profile that will minimize the probable audibility of the speed change (Figure 3-a). Since the next segment has a much stronger tempo than the current segment (0.25 vs 0.016), making any speed changes in the second half of the meld more audible than they would be in the first half, we use a speed profile that keeps this second half at the natural speed of the next segment. Figure 3-b shows the speed profile that would be used is the current segment had a stronger tempo than the next segment. Either way, the speed changes during the weak-tempo portion of the meld. This accommodation is possible using the resampling approach described in Equation 1.

With these known resampling profiles, the spectrograms can be cross-correlated to determine the best offset (in their respectively resampled timelines) to bring their beats into alignment. It is these two (resampled) beat-aligned sections that we will be melding. In a loose analogy to visual image compositing, we now know how to warp and register the two images. Next, we describe how to complete the melding.

III. Frequency-Dependent Cross-Fade using Seam Carving

At the completion of the pre-processing and alignment steps (described in the appendix), we have two time-aligned (and tempo-aligned) spectrograms. Now, we need to determine where and how to merge them. As with traditional visual seam carving, we want to transition from one spectral "texture" (the current segment) to another (the next segment) in a way that hides the transition. As with seam carving, we want the length of the "carving line" through the spectrograms to be compact in order to minimize that distortion to the underlying content. Sometimes, the best solution will be a vertical carving line, since that will give undistorted content on each side of the carve for the maximum amount of playback time. As will be shown, this simple approach will fail, however, when there is significant amounts of energy impacted by this choice.

Knowing that we are operating on spectrograms that will need to be (approximately) inverted to return to the temporal domain, we also want the transition between the spectrograms to respect the continuity needed for a valid inversion. Otherwise, when we try to invert the carved composite, we may create artificial onsets and even sharp "pops," since the desired composite does not resemble any valid magnitude spectrogram that can be accurately inverted. Therefore, instead of determining a single carve point for each spectral band, we instead determine a starting and ending time for a linear cross-fade within that band. To avoid degenerating to a single cut point, we require a minimum separation of 0.5 sec. between the start and end points.

The temporal-compactness and texture-matching constraints between the carving start-end lines can be addressed with dynamic programming. This starts with the lowest frequency bands, determines the "quality" of each possible start-end point by examining the local texture alignment: if the two underlying textures between the start-end points are similar, the quality of that pair is given a high score and the opposite if they are dissimilar. From each starting state for the lowest frequency band (where the starting state is the start-end value and its computed quality), we move to the next higher band. We do a similar evaluation on the texture alignment for this band. The combination of these, along with a penalty to the accumulating quality for non-vertical transitions in the start-end points, can be easily incorporated in the dynamic programming procedure for efficient consideration of all the possibilities.

There are two important refinements that we make to the standard dynamic-programming solution. The first refinement adjusts the approach for the fact that we expect longer coherent phase lengths in the low frequency bands. Stated another way, we expect the best transitions to be shorter (in time) at high frequencies than at low frequencies. As we move up the frequency axis with our solutions, we only penalize position changes in the start-end times that either lengthen the distance between those points, relative to the previous (lower-frequency) band, or that change the center of the cross-fade relative to its position in the previous (lower-frequency) band.

The second refinement is to group the frequency bands in a mel-scale–like spacing [17]. This greatly speeds up the time that it takes to find our proposed solution, to the point that most of the solution time is done in spectrogram inversion, even with the improvements that we discuss next. For the examples shown in this paper, we used 16 spectral bands, going up to 8 kHz.

Figure 4 shows a specific example. The overlapping portions of the two time- and tempo-aligned spectrograms are shown on the left and right sides of the figure. Using dynamic programming, we determine the best mask (center), based on the quality of the energy match within each frequency region minus the moving-center and lengthening-transition penalties described earlier. For the shown example, using that dynamic-programming–optimized selection, the left edge of the meld is the earliest overlap slice and the right edge for the bottom 14 spectral regions is at the latest overlap slice. For the top two regions the end of the cross-fade moves closer to its start. Having found these optimal start and end points, we linearly fade the spectrograms between them. Beyond the mask, the melded spectrogram is identical to the current or next spectrograms. In this example, the current spectrogram segment is used (without change) to the left of the shown regions and the next spectrogram segment is used to the right, as well as in the upper right side of the shown region.

Next, we describe localized spectrogram inversion, so we can avoid having to regenerate all of the audio samples for the full song durations.

IV. Locality-Constrained Spectrogram Inversion

After the audio is combined along the seam, we have a combined magnitude spectrogram. This includes large sections of the current and next songs that need to remain completely unchanged in the temporal domain. Note that these sections have not been altered within the combined magnitude spectrogram; however, we need to ensure that they remain unchanged in the phase/temporal domain.

This is different than the typical spectrogram inversion where we have no phase constraints but, by adding these constraints, we are able to massively reduce the amount of computation needed. Instead of having to reconstruct full (melded) songs, we only need to reconstruct the melded sections of the songs and abut those with the (truncated) original temporal waveforms. Importantly for deployment and large-scale processing, this isolates the melded regions from each other: if we want to meld together hundreds of songs, for hours of seamless music, we can easily do this in parallel, making the process (in this example) hundreds of times faster.

The change to the spectrogram inversion is to keep copies of the complex spectrograms from the current and next segments (that is, the 40 seconds at the end of the current song and the beginning of the next song that we computed in Section II. We use the full complex values as our constraint for all of the non-overlapping sections of the spectrograms: since they are not changed by our speed changes or our carving/cross-fading, those sections of the complex spectrograms remain valid and we can exactly match them by their outermost edge (where we want to splice their inverted values to the time samples of the original songs). The process is a very simple change to the classic Griffin-Lim inversion algorithm[15]:

- From a hypothesized complex spectrogram: Create a temporal sequence using the weighted overlapped-added values given by the inverse Fourier transform to the slices. This becomes your hypothesized temporal sequence.
- From a hypothesized temporal sequence: Create a complex spectrogram, using the parameters from Section II. Modify this complex spectrogram by:
    - In the areas where we do not have phase constraints, rescaling the magnitudes of the spectral components to match our melded spectrogram.
    - In the areas where we have both phase and magnitude constraints, replacing the spectral components with those dictated by those constraints.

This process is repeated until the desired quality of convergence. One additional trick that speeds the convergence is to start with a phase estimate in the melded regions that is the weighted average of the phases from those locations in the two original songs. This requires a little extra bookkeeping, since it requires keeping track of the speed profiles used in the melding but, in our experiments, it does reduce the number of iterations needed by a factor of 4-5 times. We find that we

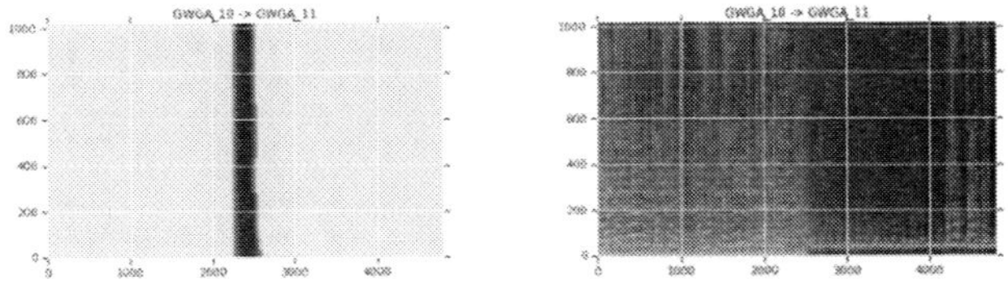

Dido "Loveless Hearts" to "Day Before We Went To War".
overlapping length: 5 sec; speed change: 4.1% increase; tempo strength: 0.031, 0.032

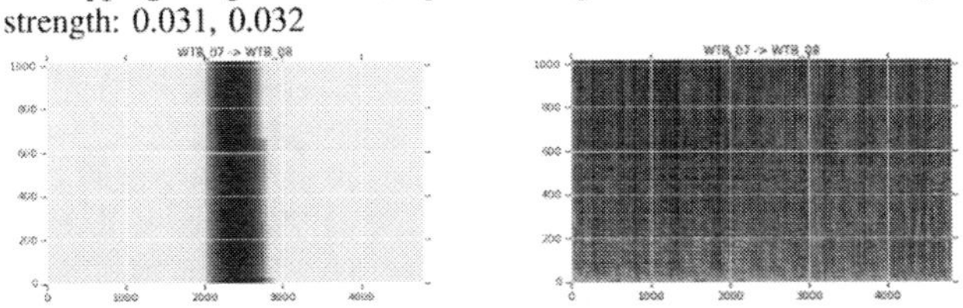

Everlast "This Kind of Lonely" to "Soul Music".
overlapping length: 11.67 sec; speed change: 4.8% increase; tempo strength: 0.028, 0.022

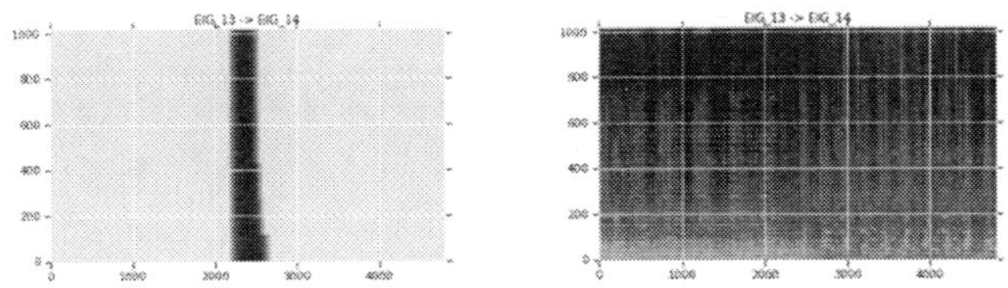

Liz Phair "Shatter" to "Flower".
overlapping length: 7.11 sec; speed change: 17.3% increase; tempo strength: 0.009, 0.029

Figure 5: Selected examples of meld transitions that were audibly indistinguishable from beat-aligned cross fading. The similarity in the two versions is to be expected, since there is no significant frequency dependence in the meld profile.

can create high quality results using this approach in 3-10 iterations, depending on the sound complexity.

V. Putting it Together: Experiments and Results

For our evaluation, we used four albums and genres from different artists: a 14-song electro-house album *In Search of Sunrise I* by DJ Tiesto, an 11-song electro-pop album *Girl Who Got Away* by Dido, a 15-song hip-hop album *White Trash Beautiful* by Everlast, and an 18-song Indie-rock album *Exile in Guyville* by Liz Phair. The evaluation was conducted in two manners. The first was a continuous listening to the full melded albums. This ensured that there were no unexpected artifacts in the full sequence that would not be observed from listening to the reconstructed music only near the transitions. The second was listening to two alternatives: the full melding result, using the approach described in the previous sections and comparing it to three simpler versions: (1) simple cross fading, (2) beat-aligned cross fading with a fixed speed profile, and (3) beat-aligned cross fading with the speed profile determined by the beat prominence. The alternatives were presented as 40-second snippets of sound, centered at the transition.

For the first test, there were no unwanted artifacts in the full album listening tests. This ensures that we were not overlooking issues in joining our (cropped) original song audio

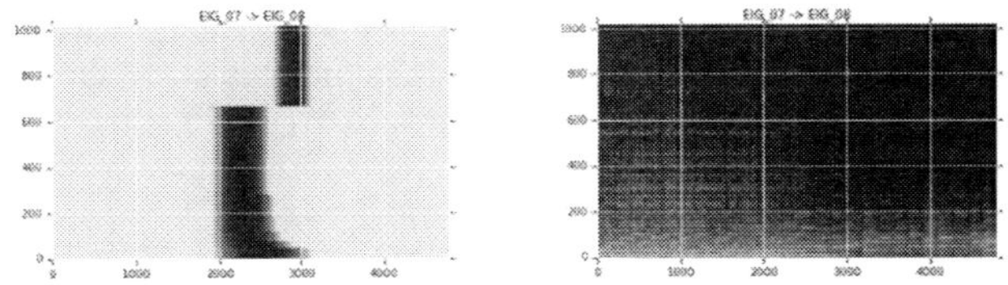

Liz Phair "Explain It To Me" to "Canary".
overlapping length: 15 sec; speed change: 2.2% increase; tempo strength: 0.029, 0.010

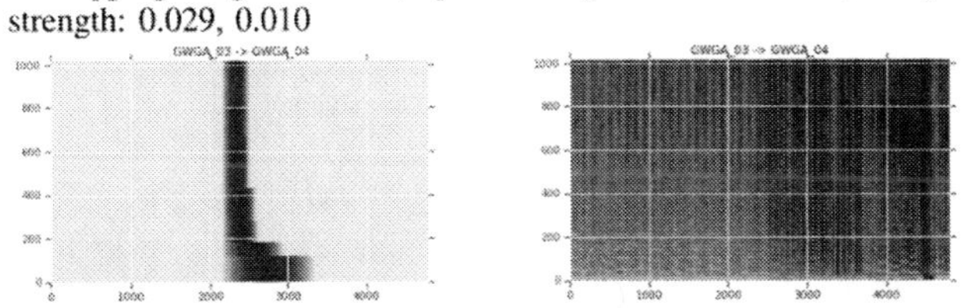

Dido "Let Us Move On" to "Blackbird".
overlapping length: 15.0 sec; speed change: 4.2% increase; tempo strength: 0.016, 0.238

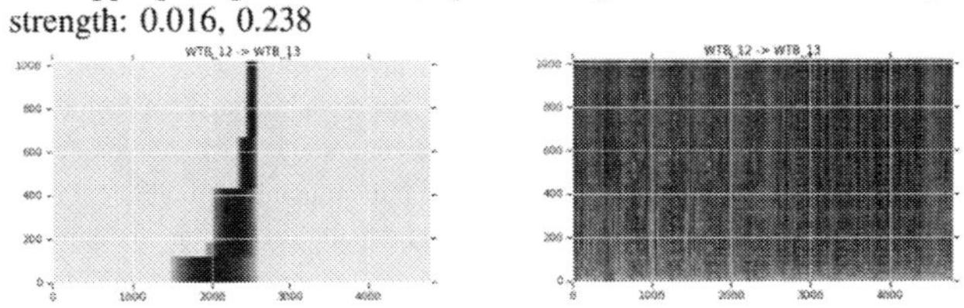

Everlast "Ticking Away" to "Pain".
overlapping length: 14.4 sec; speed change: 4.8% decrease; tempo strength: 0.054, 0.032

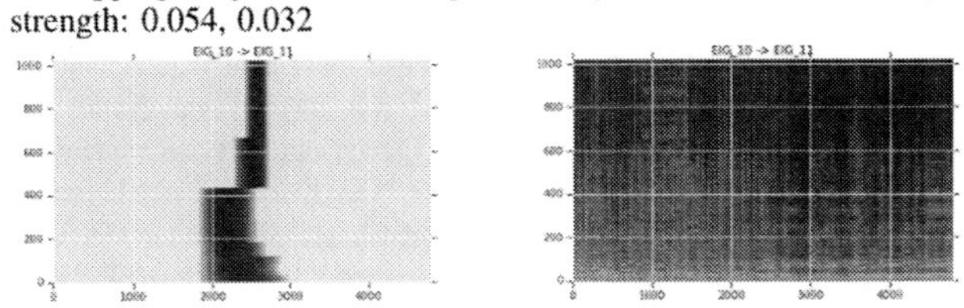

*Liz Phair "F*** and Run" to "Girls! Girls! Girls!".*
overlapping length: 14.9 sec; speed change: 5.4% decrease; tempo strength: 0.070, 0.030

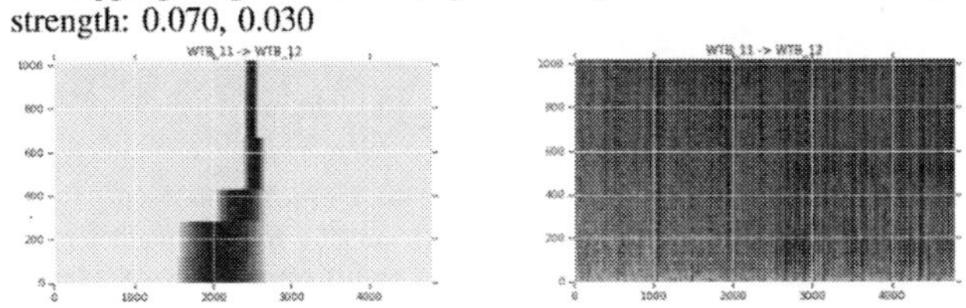

Everlast "Sad Girl" to "Ticking Away".
overlapping length: 15.0 sec; speed change: 8.3% decrease; tempo strength: 0.038, 0.040

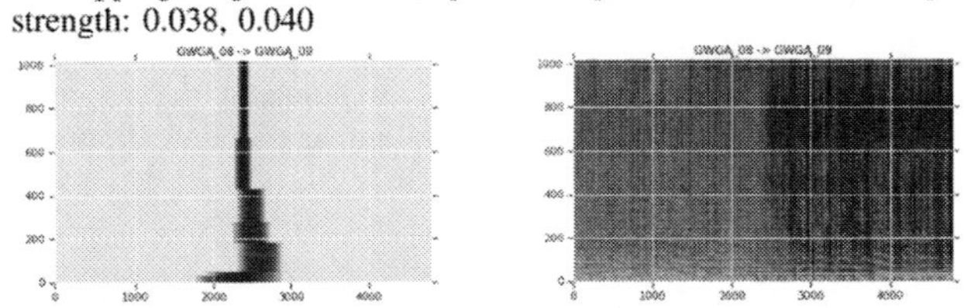

Dido "Go Dreaming" to "Happy New Year".
overlapping length: 15.0 sec; speed change: 12.1% decrease; tempo strength: 0.064, 0.112

Figure 6: Selected examples of meld transitions that were audibly better than beat-aligned cross fading. In particular, the frequency-dependent profile to the meld helps avoid muddled notes in the upper registers.

waveforms with the waveforms that we compute using our local phase-constrained spectrogram inversions of the song transitions. This validates our approach for making this feasible for large-scale deployment.

For the second test, in every case, the melded transitions were judged better than the cross fade without beat alignment. If the tempo measure is strong, simple cross fade is immediately perceived as worse, since two beats are clearly heard at offset times to each other. When the tempo measure was weak for one or both songs, the loss in quality was less extreme but there still was the impression of a "muddier" sound.

In contrast, for some transitions, we could not hear a significant difference between the melded transitions and the beat-aligned cross fades. This was especially true for the electro-house album: in these cases, the continuity of the beat through the transition completely overwhelms any finer grain evaluation. However, we also found at least some of the transitions in each of the other genres we considered were handled just as well by beat-aligned cross fades as by our melding approach. Why did this happen? Our system was able to *automatically find a nearly identical carving path* to the beat-aligned cross fade (see Figure 5). In these cases, based on the audio spectrograms, it made sense to cut the frequencies together. Since our carving penalty criteria often favors frequency-independent profiles, there was little difference between the beat-aligned cross fade and the meld in these cases.

Most importantly, however, there were many cases in which the frequency transitions should not have been done at the same time, even for beat aligned snippets. Figure 6 shows six samples from this set. Here, the transitions took on a very different profile from the straight cuts shown in Figure 5. In these cases, the melded transitions were audibly judged better than the alternatives. Qualitatively, the difference was most noticeable in how muddled the high notes of the music sounded. The melded transitions did a better job in avoiding "doubled up" notes in these higher registers.

VI. CONCLUSIONS

By combining techniques taken from visual seam carving with tempo analysis and beat alignment, we are able to create seemingly continuous musical performances from separate song recordings. Our approach allows the non-uniform cross-fading of two songs by examining where the frequencies best overlap. We are able to compute the melded waveform in a way that allows it to be used directly with the main body of the original recordings, greatly reducing the amount of computation needed in spectrogram inversion and allowing for parallel processing of long play lists.

REFERENCES

[1] A. de Mooij and W. Verhaegh, "Learning Preferences for Music Playlists," Koninklijke Philips Electronics, Tech. Rep. PR-TN 2003/00735, September 2003.

[2] Q. Lin, L. Lu, C. Weare, and F. Seide, "Music rhythm characterization with application to workout-mix generation," in International Conference on Acoustics, Speech, and Signal Processing. IEEE, March 2010, pp. 69–72.

[3] Apple, "Apple Music," 2019, https://www.apple.com/apple-music/ [accessed: 2019-10-15].

[4] YouTube, "YouTube Music," 2019, https://music.youtube.com/ [accessed: 2019-10-15].

[5] R. M. Bittner, M. Gu, G. Hernandez, E. J. Humphrey, T. Jehan, H. McCurry, and N. Montecchio, "Automatic playlist sequencing and transitions," in International Society for Music Information Retrieval Conference, October 2017, pp. 442–448.

[6] C. Lestoc, "Automatically mix songs with these 5 software solutions," 2018, http://www.windowsreport.com/automatically-mix-songs-software [accessed: 2019-10-15].

[7] D. Cliff, "Hang the DJ: Automatic sequencing and seamless mixing of dance-music tracks," HP Labs Technical Report, vol. 104, 2000.

[8] T. Hirai, H. Doi, and S. Morishima, "Musicmixer: Computer-aided DJ system based on an automatic song mixing," in International Conference on Advances in Computer Entertainment Technology, ser. ACE '15. New York, NY, USA: ACM, 2015, pp. 41:1–41:5.

[9] S. Avidan and A. Shamir, "Seam carving for content-aware image resizing," in ACM SIGGRAPH. New York, NY, USA: ACM, 2007.

[10] P. Soille, "Morphological image compositing," IEEE Transactions on Pattern Analysis and Machine Intelligence, vol. 28, no. 5, May 2006, pp. 673–683.

[11] H. Gu, Y. Yu, and W. Sun, "A new optimal seam selection method for airborne image stitching," in International Workshop on Imaging Systems and Techniques. IEEE, May 2009, pp. 1000 – 1014.

[12] L. Yu, E.-J. Holden, M. C. Dentith, and H. Zhang, "Towards the automatic selection of optimal seam line locations when merging optical remote-sensing images," International Journal of Remote Sensing, vol. 33, no. 4, 2012, pp. 1000–1014.

[13] W. Zhang, B. Guo, M. Li, X. Liao, and W. Li, "Improved seam-line searching algorithm for uav image mosaic with optical flow," Sensors (Basel), vol. 18, no. 4, April 2018, p. 1214.

[14] R. Szeliski, "Image alignment and stitching: A tutorial," Foundations and Trends in Computer Graphics and Vision, vol. 2, no. 1, 2006, pp. 1–104.

[15] D. Griffin and J. Lim, "Signal estimation from modified short-time Fourier transform," Transactions on Acoustics, Speech, and Signal Processing, vol. 32, no. 2, 1984, pp. 236–243.

[16] G. Tzanetakis and G. Percival, "An effective, simple tempo estimation method based on self-similarity and regularity," in International Conference on Acoustics, Speech, and Signal Processing. IEEE, May 2013, pp. 241–245.

[17] S. S. Stevens, J. Volkmann, and E. B. Newman, "A scale for the measurement of the psychological magnitude pitch," The Journal of the Acoustical Society of America, vol. 8, no. 3, January 1937, pp. 185–190.

[18] SciPy.org, "numpy.hanning," 2019, http://docs.scipy.org/doc/numpy/reference/generated/numpy.hanning.html [accessed: 2019-10-15].

APPENDIX
TEMPO MATCHING AND SEGMENT-LEVEL ALIGNMENT

Our system operates on the spectrograms of the end/start of the songs that we are melding. After silence trimming, we compute the spectrogram on the last/first 40 seconds of each track. We use a frame length of 50 ms, extracted by a Hanning window [18], with factor of four overlap (*i.e.*, a 12.5-ms step between frames). The FFT size that is used is the next power of two greater than twice the frame length: for example, using a sample rate of 16,000 samples per second, the FFT size is 2048. If the underlying audio rate is greater than 16,000 samples/sec, we do the full bandwidth transform to generate spectrograms that will be used during the inversion process. For the sake of computational efficiency and reproducibility we do most of our processing on the bottom 8 kHz of the spectrogram.

To estimate the tempo, we start from $\rho[l]$, the correlation coefficient for each segment lag, l (Figure 2 left). While peaks can be seen in $\rho[l]$, the profiles are still often very noisy, making it difficult to determine the best candidate beat duration. To overcome this limitation, we compute a sub-harmonically reinforced, differential tempo measure, $t[l]$, from $\rho[l]$:

$$t[l] = \frac{1}{N_l}\sum_{i=1}^{N_l} \rho[il] - (m_\rho[i-1,l] + m_\rho[i,l])/2$$

$$m_\rho[j,l] = \min_{k=jl+1}^{(j+1)l-1} \rho[k]$$

The measure is locally (in the lag space) differential since, for a lag l, it uses the strength difference in $\rho[il]$ at the ith sub-harmonic of l and the minimum values of ρ within one period on either side, reducing the main lobe effect seen in the auto-correlation function and suppressing halved tempos. Sub-harmonic re-enforcement is provided by these difference values on integer multiples of a fundamental period. When there is a consistent tempo, this differential measure brings the tempo peaks into sharp relief. With this differential measure, 0.25 is a very strong beat and below 0.01 corresponds to a weak or inconsistent tempo. Therefore, for each of the current/next tempo curves we collect the lags and strengths of all of the peaks that are above 0.01 and above both of its closest neighbor lags. We use these two sets of candidate tempos and strengths ($\{T_C[k]\}$ and $\{S_c[k]\}$ for the current segment and $\{T_N[k]\}$ and $\{S_N[k]\}$ for the next segment) to determine how we will change the speeds of the segments to allow for beat alignment.

We look across all the pairs of $T_C[k_C]$ and $T_N[k_N]$ to find the pair that gives the strongest combined strength $S[k_C, k_N] = S_c[k_C] + S_N[k_N]$ with the least noticeable speed change $\gamma[k_c, k_N] = T_C[k_C]/T_N[k_N] - 1$. To balance these criteria, we first collect all of the (k_C, k_N) pairings which give a speed change (γ) within a user-specified allowed range (*e.g.*, -15% - 25%) and penalize the combined strength by the perceptible speed change: $S[k_C, k_N] \times (1 - \max(0, |\gamma[k_c, k_n]| - \gamma_{thres}))$ where γ_{thres} is, for example, 5%.

Our final result from this stage is a speed change γ as well as the maximum strengths of tempo peaks seen in each song, $S_{\gamma,C} = \max\{S_C\}$ and $S_{\gamma,N} = \max\{S_N\}$. We know that, to match the tempos using this pairing, we need to play the current segment at $\gamma + 1$ of the speed of the next segment. We use the maximum tempo strengths to determine the profile for that speed change, over the course of the overlapping sections, since a speed change in the stronger-tempo segment will be more noticeable than that in the weaker-tempo segment.

Given the relative speeds we need to use to match the tempo of our current and next segments, we could explicitly resample one segments using a constant speed of $1+\gamma$ (if resampling the current segment) or $\frac{1}{1+\gamma}$ (if resampling the next segment). However, for minimal detectability, we want the speed transition to smoothly move from the natural speed of the current segment (at the start of the meld) to the natural speed of the next segment (by the end of the meld). We know that speed changes are more easily heard in segments with strong beats; therefore, we bias the transition to maintain the segment with the stronger beat at its natural speed for a longer interval.

To do this we create a target speed profile, like that shown in Figure 3. We allow the speed transition to happen over between half and the full overlapping section, to reduce the perceptibility of the speed change on segments with a strong tempo: when a strong tempo is present, we keep the speed at that segments natural speed for up to half of the transition length. We do ensure that at least half of the transition length is used to go from the current to the next natural speed, to avoid abrupt changes. We use $S_{\gamma,C}$ and $S_{\gamma,N}$ in determining the relative lengths of constant speed sections (if any), R_C and R_N according to:

$$R_{C,\max} = 0.5 * \frac{S_{\gamma,C}}{S_{max}} \qquad R_{N,\max} = 0.5 * \frac{S_{\gamma,N}}{S_{max}}$$

$$R_C = \max(0, \min(R_{C,\max} - \epsilon, \frac{0.5 * R_{C,\max}}{R_{C,\max} + R_{N,\max}}))$$

$$R_N = \max(0, \min(R_{N,\max} - \epsilon, \frac{0.5 * R_{N,\max}}{R_{C,\max} + R_{N,\max}}))$$

$$\epsilon = 0.5 * \frac{S_{min}}{S_{max}}$$

R_C and R_N are (respectively) the fraction of the overlapping section that is played back at the current- and next-segment's natural speed. In between, we linearly change speed for the remaining $1 - R_C - R_N$ fraction of the overlap.

This set of constraints on speed, along with $L_{F,C}$ the natural overlap duration on the current segment, fully determines the (re-sampled) tempo-aligned duration L_F according to:

$$L_F = round(\frac{L_{F,C}}{(1.0 + 0.5 * \gamma * (1.0 + R_N - R_C))}) \quad (1)$$

With this number of samples on the target speed profile (Figure 3), the natural-speed duration in the current segment is $L_{F,C}$ and in the next segment is $L_{F,N} = \frac{L_{F,C}}{1+\gamma}$.

For computational efficiency, we form a (doubly) time-dependent dot-product matrix, showing the spectral product of the current and next segments at those (current- and next-segment) natural times. The dot product is over the spectral bands but not over time, to allow us to consider different full-transition durations on our speed profile.

To enforce our $1+\gamma$ relative speeds, we integrate our dot-product matrix on lines with a $1+\gamma$ slope and with an intercept determined by the offset time between the current and next segment. On that line, we sample the integral using the sampling profile given by Figure 3. The sample spacing is one unit on the vertical (current-segment-time) axis when the playback speed is the current segment's natural speed and is one unit on the horizontal (next-segment-time) axis when the playback speed is the next segment's natural speed (with intermediate spacings for intermediate speeds).

Since the dot-product matrix is being computed on products of spectral amplitudes (so, non-negative components), we also normalize the line-integral value that we get by the separate power profiles of the resampled overlapping sections, giving a correlation-coefficient measure.

Using this approach, we find the offset with the strongest correlation coefficient. We use that offset, with the sampling profiles to generate the two underlying tempo-aligned, offset-aligned sections that we will be melding. Section III describes the process that we use to complete the melding.

Promoting Fluency of Streaming Video by Learning Human Perceptive Traits to Reveal the Vital Section in Outstanding Quality

Chiang Shu Chiao
Department of Computer Science and Engineering
Waseda University
Tokyo, Japan
e-mail: csc19950207@dcl.cs.waseda.ac.jp

Tatsuo Nakajima
Department of Computer Science and Engineering
Waseda University
Tokyo, Japan
e-mail: tatsuo@dcl.cs.waseda.ac.jp

***Abstract* — Currently, the quality of digital media and the quantity of contents are both increasing rapidly. For instance, watching e-sport competitions often suffers from unstable bandwidth, which causes the video to stutter or have a low resolution. In this situation, users will have a negative experience. Many situations can cause problems of congestion in real-time applications or 3D displays. To solve this kind of problem, we attempt to determine an inverse solution according to the path. This project adopts a reverse operation that reduces necessary data but maintains the same quality perception of user experience by utilizing the characteristics of the human vision and brain. To explore our approach, we develop a prototype that changes the resolution of the image according to a user's habit and shows the part in focus clearly while leaving the resolution of the background lower. It selects interested sub-image in pictures and only displays them with higher quality to achieve a lower transmission requirement. This optimization will allow the user experience smoother streaming when there is congestion or unstable situations. Then, we conduct a preliminary user study to investigate some future directions and explore some potential flaws.**

Keywords -- Image processing; deep learning; accelerated streaming; media data structure.

I. INTRODUCTION

Regardless of whether virtual or real, required resolution is steadily increasing. Moreover, many applications tend to develop the 3D aspect, which requires many times the data flow of 2D [7]. Therefore, extracting significant areas will create an efficient method to reduce congestion and instantly increase demand. For example, in real-time sport races, there may be many people linking at the same time despite it not being a busy period. In that case, the user may experience intermittent loading or a low resolution screen, as shown in Figure 1. Even when communication equipment provides greater bandwith, the data requirement will also increase with the bandwidth due to more devices linking or a larger data consumption cost. As an analogy, building more roads is not the solution to traffic jams, and changing the usage habit of transportation is necessary [1].

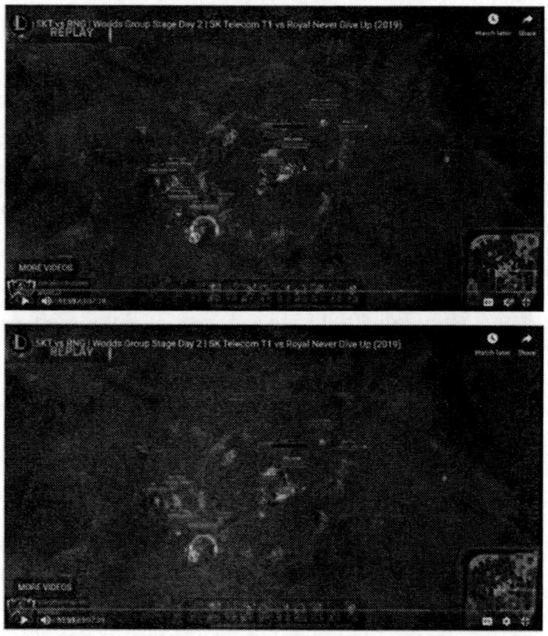

Figure 1. The top is a screenshot at 1080p, and the buttom is a screenshot at 240p. When users view these on large size monitors, they obviously note the differences between their sharpness [9]

If we can provide a more fluent model, it relieves pressure for route and improves performance. In addition, in 3D, we create a hypothetical scenario. In the future, car windows may have augmented reality services, as shown in Figure 2, which can show the information about landmarks, stores, or traffic warnings. However, drivers may not want to display all things all the time, so we can predict the driver's interest and show what he/she needs at that moment. In general, we also want to use it in movies, but it will be very difficult to recognize, identify, and filter images because every scene will have underlying connotations that are open to interpretation.

Figure 2. Showing out the concept map of car window equips the AR device [10]

This paper presents a system that will show everything in best quality that the bandwidth allows. When the network transmission volume decreases, it will turn on a system to sort the hierarchy of subobjects, collect a user's eye gaze on the screen, find the area where the user is looking and train the personal interest database by collecting gaze information. For the purpose of assuring the video can run smoothly in any situations with the same perception to its user, it can also record the effect on the user after using this system. Based on the above approach, we can determine how to enhance this prototype.

The remainder of the paper is structured as follows. Section 2 presents the information about researches that are related to the human's usage of multiple media and papers which study the human perceptive influence from media. In addition, we compare it with current model to find out the adventage of this idea. Section 3 expresses the method how we process this problem and proposes a new structure for this anticipation. This includes the work in the integral architecture and individual steps. Section 4 describes the implementation. In section 5, we list the main feedback collected from investigations. Last, we make a brief summary and indicate the feasible future work.

II. RELATED WORK

Scientists have studied human visual attention for decades. Some of them focus on understanding the image data. Others tried to understand the temporal effect of eye motion in videos. Others have attempted to understand the behavior within the shot and build a high-level theory. Since then, considerable progress in image saliency has been proposed, but less work has been performed on video saliency. Some researchers working on video saliency have built methods by narrowing the thought focus to a small frame of candidate gaze location or having a higher result by transitioning over time in the video field [2].

In addition to the interaction of viewing and video display, considerable information needs to be considered; visual attention is not limited to analyzing pictures or image processing. The aim of an objective image quality assessment is used to evaluate the quality of pictures or videos as a human observer. Previous studies have investigated the content of pictures related to human behavior [3]. However, machine learning technologies have flourished recently. This shows better performance in processing human traits [4]. In previous researches on this issue, most studies determine users' interests by analyzing their habits or studying which image or region attracts people's attention. We now change to the deep learning method to find the target.

Recent models almost use "adaptive bitrate streaming" technology to solve the problem of automatically adjusting video quality. Thus, image resolution also plays an important role here, and the resolution of streaming media shown is dependent on the network speed. Image resolution finds the best fit pixels of the frame for the client, so there are many different thresholds for increasing or decreasing the storage database [5]. We propose a modification to this structure such that the new units will not be the frame but a sub-image of the frame with position information [6].

This work will integrate the above benefits; leading to an application evolved to another level that has more interaction with humans.

III. METHOD

The basic flow in the proposed method is shown in Figure 3. The process requires obtaining the video at the beginning. First, video is placed in filters to segment and crop the image into several sub slices from a complete frame. Then, the eye gaze is obtained to indicate areas that are interesting to the user. Third, those images are saved into a data pool. Next, we compare the trained deep learning database and record the user's private interest orientation. Finally, a client part saves the information, and another server part is established to save those sliced images. Finally, the processed video is shown according to the above steps.

A. *Segment / crop image*

In the first step, matrix operations need to be conducted, such as 1) shifting to reduce the gradient and trivial pixels in a single picture, 2) blurring the original image to make it simpler to capture, 3) fuzzing color blocks to create a boundary and 4) making preliminarily analyzing the image. Then, the raw information is roughly combined with the results to crop the main objects of video. This makes it easier to distinguish each item in the frame. Then, those target areas are defined in boxes, and their location information is noted (Figure 4a). These details are recorded in a temporary list for comparison with eye gaze location. The next step describes how to obtain the eye gaze location.

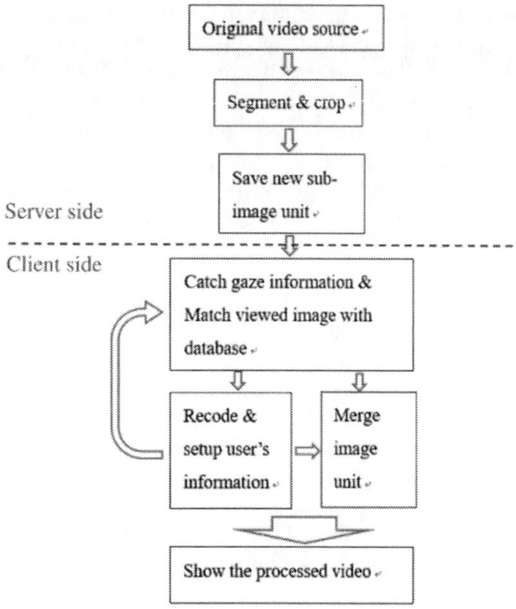

Figure 3. This is the basic system flow that demostrates how to process raw video and the design of data structure arrangement

B. Catch the gaze

The proposed design will learn what part is suitable for a user. Therefore, this step is combined with the first step. After we conduct the initial process that segments out sub-objects in the screen, it obtains the user's gaze to select where the main interesting object is, which has to be packaged in each frame (Figure 4b). Then, only an interested area is showed in high quality, but comprehensive perception is still close to a full high quality picture (Figure 4c). So, the total required data is significantly less than the original full high quality picture. The selected object is stored in the database and will have priority if the same object appears again. This work helps us train the database to recognize the same object at a later time. The information also promotes the efficiency of segmenting and cropping images. Therefore, the first and second steps are mutually optimized.

C. Match / classify label

We match those selected sub-images to the real underlying meanings; just as many things in the real world are rich in meaning, it will change according to cultural practices [8]. Thus, we should define some similar items in the set and then teach the machine to know which meanings are the same will be another challenge. There are two main works that need to be completed here. One is defining a new cluster when we identify an object that cannot be classified in the existing set. The other is assigning the object to the correct set (Figure 4d). These studies will require deep learning technology, as mentioned above, so that the system will be able to more quickly and efficiently recognize and analyze underlying messages in the real world. We want to find a positive method for labeling them. The next section explains these steps in more detail.

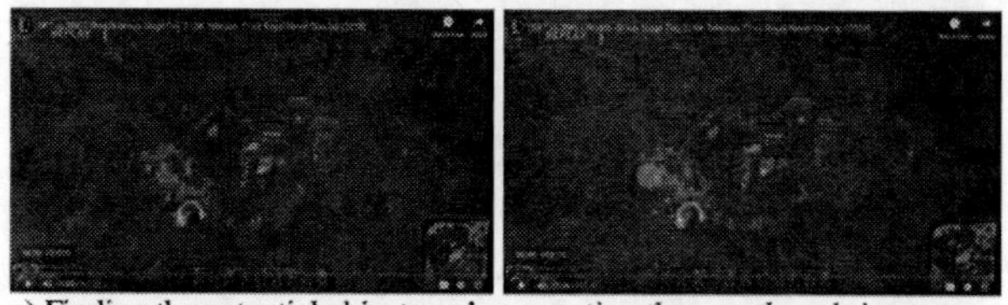

a) Finding the potential objects and segmenting them as the sub-image
b) Getting the gaze information

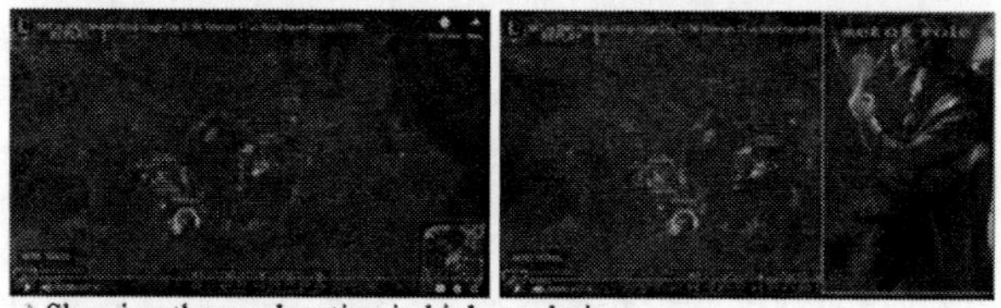

c) Showing the eye location in high resolution
d) Matching with database to build the user's interest pool

Figure 4. Descripting the detail of each section [11][12]

D. Build database

This is the main part of the previous section because building the label set is the principal challenge. The difficult part is that many things have the same meaning but not the same appearance. We need to teach the machine to recognize them, create a new set from the data pool, and find the characteristics of each set for classification. When we match new slices, it needs to mark those features because we use "feature matching" to compare the selected object and the sets in the database. At high speeds, which are often necessary, it is compared with only the common features of each set. Therefore, feature extraction will be trained by deep learning, which imitates how humans recognize an item, similar to how humans can rapidly determine implications from small clues.

E. Storage strategy

First, some basic concepts should be understood. We should learn how videos are saved in current streaming platforms. Currently, general frames are saved as complete pictures in different hierarchies of pixel levels. Frames are defined as the basic unit of a video. However, this system will require a slight change so that it mitigates the unit to the sub-object, so we need more space to record them or store those sub-objects separately at the beginning. Both plans need to increase one dimension to link the data to others. When the sensor detects a fluctuation in bandwidth, it changes the resolution to gradually decrease from the object of interest. The system presented in the paper needs a complex structure to store data and labels because it has considerable information in each frame. Then, we determine which type of strategy is suitable for this idea.

IV. EXPERIMENT

This work was developed in the environment of Ubuntu 18.4, OpenCV3 and Python3. Currently, the basic function of the experimental work has completed. This includes distinguishing out different things that include the features of filtering out the trivial color of images, segmenting out sub images by bounding the features of objects and cropping them out within a minimum frame box. Next, it matches the gaze locate to find the focus location and record the information back to a server for the purpose of iterative data updating. Then, we use the prepared deep learning database which is built by the Keras library in TensorFlow2. It would analyze pre-processed target pictures with the image sets in the database and list out results (figure 5b). However, auto-expansion of the image set is necessary for future work. This prototype can also track and collect users' gaze information (Figure 5a), in order to make more effective predictions according to the users' habit.

We built the version for a user study. We set up the foremost stable database to represent the deep learning set and used the mouse to replace a gaze tracker because it has better accuracy and a direct read media source. Others have used the same structure and operation as we described above.

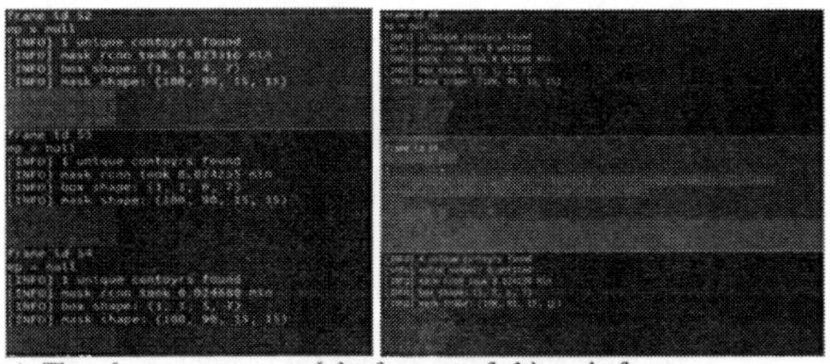

a) The advance process and the forecast of objects in frame
b) Merging the gaze information into procedure

Figure 5. The print out of surveying vision

V. PRELIMINARY USER STUDY

In this section, we present some simple questions to the participants in the user study. 1) How does the display compare with general videos? 2) Does this application help you? 3) Which part should be promoted to increase user interest? 4) How does the participant respond after we show the demo version, which includes an introduction of the concept and a trial of the prototype, depend on their career (programmer, video editor and common user).

First, we provide a survey to the programmers. After they used the system, they described two main concerns. They considered the speed to not be truly immediate. If this technology is going to work on real-time video, this problem needs to be solved. Therefore, we consider the main part where work on analyzing, segmenting and cropping should be built on the server part because those operations require very advanced devices to achieve real-time streaming. Only gaze tracking and data collection should be embedded in the client part. Then, we push this system to mobile devices because mobile devices have lower efficiency CPUs. Reaching the real-time goal will be the most significant challenge. Additionally, this system may sometimes ignore the supporting cast in favor of the main characters. This results in the related matters being ignored as well. The link between objects is too weak, which creates this defect. It is also a serious problem in general videos. Movies, music and videos all contain many meanings within every sub-image. However, the shooting technique is a topic for another paper. There are some scattered doubts, such as reducing segmentation in each frame, enlarging the minimum segment size, using a decreasing method to show the resolution around the main object from high to low, or implementing this technology in the gaming field.

We investigated a group of video creators. For these creators, the content of their videos is of utmost priority. Because media is the method through which they express their thoughts, they want to completely convey their ideas to the viewer. Therefore, when those potential users consider how the system works, they assess whether this technology would affect their product. Thus, they concentrate on object weight calculation and the weight of interactors in the feedback. For example, there is a scene of a competition in which we want to know the main object and the competitor. There are some comments that indicate that the system should provide a function for the creator to set the weight when they edit the video. Thus, the creator can have better control of the connotations that they want to display to the viewer instead of ranking the weight by users' preferences, as it may cause communication errors. They were also interested in whether this system would create benefits for the video editor. For example, rendering the video to a normal format requires considerable time and storage. If this new video storage method can speed up the process, it would be welcomed by video creators. This potential application may lead to some innovations. How it combines with video editing or optimizing rendering functions would be another use for this system.

Finally, we surveyed some general users. For those participants, we described using scenarios in real-time, live shows, and dynamic videos in social network services. This feedback contained more varied opinions. The most common question was whether 5G will solve this problem. Of course, 5G offers more bandwidth to the user, then it will enable full high quality video transmission more smoothly, but the users suspect that the hypothesis would be achieved because new services will easily exhaust its bandwidth as mentioned before. So, we consider that our approach can be used as better countermeasure. Other comments were about psychological issues, such as a live sporting race, which can also be viewed on a TV using cable to obtain data. If the network is not running well, the users have another choice, or the video can be pre-downloaded in high quality so that they do not need to watch it in real-time; thus, only live video would unavoidably fall into that case. Even in the case in which clients want to save data, telecommunications providers also provide unlimited data options if they do not truly care about the fee. Therefore, only the user who wants to watch live when many others are watching, or the network is being intensively used would require this system. Otherwise, this system will be more beneficial for mobile users or if it can provide a function that allows the user to select the size of the high-quality area. However, this system also has interesting uses in 3D space. For instance, in the scenario we mentioned before, one application would be on car windows and could determine where the driver is looking. It has positive benefits to the driver or passengers,

In sum, general users were surprised at this idea. It can filter the important information for them. This fresh idea earned more interest from the general user. Therefore, these plans may become a future blueprint.

VI. Conclusion

Our goal is going to propose a new architecture for streaming video that can play media more fluently in any situation. Based on this plan, we develop a prototype with several features to achieve it. This prototype equips functions to process the raw material which include parsing objects inside each frame, segmenting out those items and storing their information with crops. Then, we also make it can detect gaze positon to collect and track users' traits. Based on both elements, we have sources to do some approximate predictions for increasing users' perception. And, we build the deep learning database to practice it by Keras. In the experimental drill, we improve some small flaws to make it have better performance. Following from that, we will research how to execute this application with low efficacy consumption and transplant it into 3D environment. Next paragraph shows the achievement and comment of our idea. After this prototype is finished and a more complete user study is completed, this system will have considerable potential to be utilized in different aspects. There are still many sub-features that are needed to make it complete. For example, the training of deep learning database still needs to be considered because this prototype is using the prepared data source. However, the training source needs to come from multiple usage habits for making the system practical. So, how to integrate the data from users will be another problem. We should perform some studies to better understand how human perception detects objects on the screen so that we can offer more effective applications that can also run on mobile devices. There is still a long way to go before mobile hardware can match the performance of the high-end computers. Therefore, determining which part is the most helpful and transplanting this system will be a significant procedure for increasing the usage of this system. It is both a challenge and opportunity if we can simplify its operation such that it does not need to rely on advanced GPUs. It will be an innovation in the image processing field.

References

[1] J. Gehl, "Cities for People", Island Press, First Edition, 2010

[2] D. Rudoy, D. B. Goldman, El.Shechtman and L. Zelnik-Manor, "Learning Video Saliency from Human Gaze Using Candidate Selection", The IEEE Conference on Computer Vision and Pattern Recognition (CVPR), 2013, pp. 1147-1154

[3] A. Ninassi, O. Le Meur, P. Le Callet and D. Barba, "Does where you Gaze on an Image Affect your Perception of Quality? Applying Visual Attention to Image Quality Metric", IEEE International Conference on Image Processing, 12 November 2007

[4] M. Stewart, "The Actual Difference Between Statistics and Machine Learning", Medium, 2018

[5] X. Artigas, J. Ascenso, M. Dalai, S. Klomp, D. Kubasov and M. Ouaret, "The DISCOVER codec: Architecture, Techniques and Evaluation", In Proceedings of the Picture Coding Symposium (PCS'07), Lisbon, November 2007

[6] W. B. Boyle, "Method and apparatus for storing a stream of video data on a storage medium", US7657149B2, United States, 2000R.

[7] O-Y. Kwon and H-H. Heo, "Apparatus and method for 3d image conversion and a storage medium, US8977036B2, United States, 2011

[8] M. Bang, "Picture This – how pictures work", In Perception and composition, Chronicle Books, 20

[9] https://www.youtube.com/watch?v=JAKQAAxNvvc, 2019/10/19

[10] https://www.blippar.com/blog, 2019/10/07

[11] https://www.youtube.com/watch?v=JAKQAAxNvvc, 2019/10/19

[12] https://leagueoflegends.fandom.com/wiki/Twisted_Fate, 2019/10/21

Motion Analysis Using Machine Learning for Vocational Training Support

Haruka Kataoka
Graduate Student in Architecture
Polytechnic University
Kodaira-shi, Tokyo
e-mail: m19403@uitec.ac.jp

Masahiro Yokoyama, Masaki Endo, Norikatsu Fujita,
Hideyo Tsukazaki
Division of Core Manufacturing
Polytechnic University
Kodaira-shi, Tokyo
e-mail: m-yokoyama@uitec.ac.jp, endo@uitec.ac.jp,
fujita@uitec.ac.jp, tukazaki@uitec.ac.jp

Hiroshi Ishikawa
Graduate School of System Design
Tokyo Metropolitan University
Hino-shi, Tokyo
e-mail: ishikawa-hiroshi@tmu.ac.jp

Abstract—**Recently in the construction industry, because of the declining number of new employees and the aging of skilled workers, carpentry skills have not progressed. One means of transferring these skills smoothly is to train carpenter technicians at vocational skill development facilities. Nevertheless, it is difficult to spend much time at the basic tasks of carpenters, which include sharpening, chiseling, sawing, planing, and nailing, at such facilities. The development of an effective teaching method for carpentry work is desired. Therefore, we constructed a machine learning system to measure and evaluate the movements of unskilled workers. This study uses movements of skilled technicians and a questionnaire survey to evaluate the developed teaching method for tacit knowledge, i.e., intuition or knack, related to planing work.**

Keywords- Big data analysis; Carpenter skill; Component; Motion analysis; Planing work

I. INTRODUCTION

Structural forms of Japanese buildings include wooden structures, steel structures, reinforced concrete structures, and reinforced concrete structures. Among detached houses, according to data compiled by the Ministry of Land, Infrastructure, Transport and Tourism Construction statistics survey report 2018 [1], the percentage of wooden houses among detached houses exceeds 80%. Therefore, the wooden structure shown in Figure 1 represents the mainstream.

In areas where wood suitable for building materials is not available, such as the Middle East, masonry is commonly used to support buildings with walls made of brick or earth. Japanese structures use abundant timber. In addition, buildings are supported by columns and beams. However, the population of Japanese carpenters who produce and maintain wooden houses is declining precipitously. According to the Census Statistics Bureau, Ministry of Internal Affairs and Communications in 1975 [2], and a similar survey conducted in 2015 [3], the construction carpenter technician population has dropped by more than half in 45 years: from 852,745 carpenters in 1975 to only 353,980 carpenters in 2015. Specifically examining the age structure, the proportion of 15–39 year old people responsible for the future of the industry in 1975 was about 60%. By 2015 it had dropped considerably to about 20%.

Figure 1. Japanese wooden house.

The situation described above has come to represent the ordinary state of affairs. Therefore, the architectural carpentry industry must confront challenges hindering the passage of skills to inexperienced workers. One reason for this acute necessity might be that a longer time necessary to acquire full-time construction skills after starting a job engenders a lower retention rate and a higher turnover rate. Therefore, acquiring and passing on skills efficiently and rapidly can contribute greatly to improving the employment rate of young people and to lowering of the turnover rate, in addition to helping to resolve shortages of human resources.

One means of transferring these skills smoothly is to train carpenter technicians at vocational ability development facilities. Vocational training at a vocational ability development facility is intended to develop and improve abilities by enabling students to acquire the necessary knowledge and skills for a profession. Because of recent diversification of employment, vocational development facilities must impart more knowledge and skills. Nevertheless, it is difficult to spend much time at the carpenter's basic work in Japanese architecture, such as sharpening, chiseling, sawing, planing, and nailing. Therefore, an educational method must be developed that can teach carpentry work effectively in a short time.

Planing work, which makes a wood surface smooth and glossy, is often applied to pillars in a Japanese-style room where the pillars are exposed. The planing work emphasized in this study is performed mainly on two pillars, as shown in Figure 1. This skill is particularly important for Japanese carpenters: improperly performed planing work can leave wood splintery and dangerous; also, roughly finished pillars will destroy the unique atmosphere of a Japanese room.

From surveys of technical explanations and research papers published in Japan to date, we have learned the knack of planing work and how to teach related skills. In addition, a questionnaire survey related to planing work was administered to skilled workers to elicit planing work tips from workers. We also analyzed skilled and unskilled workers' behaviors during planing work. Differences were clarified from motion analysis results [4],[5].

A huge amount of work and a great deal of time are necessary to compare motion analysis results manually. Conducting training efficiently requires rapid analysis of training data and provision of feedback promptly to trainees. Therefore, for this study, we are examining improvement of training efficiency using a system that analyzes and visualizes big data related to skills that can be acquired during training. As described herein, we summarize the possibility of training effects by machine learning in the field of vocational training based on analysis using k-means method for planing work training data.

The remainder of the paper is organized as follows. Section II presents earlier research related to this topic. In Section III, we propose a K-means analytical method using data collected for planing work. Section IV presents a description of experimentally obtained results for our proposed method and a discussion of the results. Section V is a summary of the study contributions and expectations for future work.

II. RELATED WORK

Chen et al. conducted a series of studies specifically examining motion analysis related to carpentry skills [6]–[8]. The studies and the results are described below.

In one study [6], Chen et al. analyzed the same planing work as that examined in this study. They specifically reported details of measurement results of one of the four skilled workers. Results indicated that the posture during work should be "half-body"(diagonally opposite to the planing material). Half body is a posture similar to that shown in Figure 2, which portrays the posture with one leg before a half step from a standing position.

Figure 2. Half body (diagonally opposite to the planing material).

They were able to classify planing work into four basic forms: a providing planing motion, a cutting motion produced by rapid closing of the elbow, a cutting motion resulting from a large backward movement, and sudden stopping of the planing motion.

Chen et al. used a motion capture system to analyze sawing operations [7]. The report describes comparison of the sawing behaviors of skilled and unskilled persons. Results highlight their differences during work in terms of the forehead position, right arm movement, and saw speed. However, that report presented an analysis of few data. Its results are therefore regarded as being less generalizable. Features common to skilled people and those common to unskilled people were not described. Moreover, the analysis of measured values used no objective method such as an analytical statistical method or a clustering method.

Research using a Kinect™ device (Microsoft Corp.) for motion analysis includes one study described by Kurebayashi et al. [8] with a developed system that can animate skeletal information measured using Kinect™. Furthermore, the system was used for a junior high school class: evaluations of the students' feelings of use were assessed, showing high evaluations. Nevertheless, classification and organization of student motions were not performed using data obtained from this system.

As described above, several behavioral analyses related to carpentry skills have been conducted, but results of only a few test subjects have been presented. Moreover, no objective method has been applied for data analysis. An earlier report [9] explaining various methods used to analyze big data is helpful for selecting an analytical method for big data obtained from many subjects, as in this study. Therefore, this study examines whether a difference between skilled and unskilled workers can be extracted by application of the K-means method, a clustering method, to results obtained from numerous test subjects.

III. Our Proposed Method

This section presents a description of a method for analyzing data with machine learning using training data from planing work.

A. Data collection

In the experiment, the subject completed eight consecutive planing work bouts over the entire length of the work material. The subject's movements were measured using a Kinect™ sensor. In addition, the force generated during the work was measured using a strain gauge load cell (capacity 500 N). Figure 3 portrays the positional relation and axes for Kinect™ and the test subject.

Kinect™ is prone to misrecognize skeletal information when measuring from a perspective that includes overlapping of body parts (e.g., the position information of the right and left elbows is switched). Therefore, Kinect™ was installed to give a perspective by which the body parts overlap to the least extent possible during operations, thereby mitigating misrecognition. The relation between the load direction and the axis during the planing operation is designated as the X axis; the pulling force is along the Y axis, with pushing force also occurring along the horizontal axis. The Z axis shows pushing force in the vertical direction.

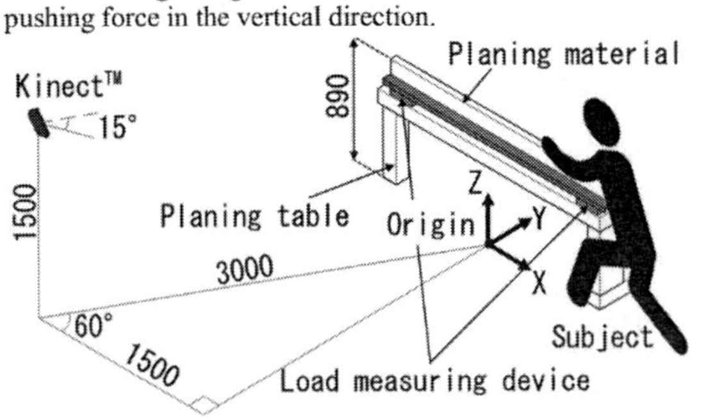

Figure 3. Kinect™ and the subject's positional relation and axes (unit: mm).

The work material was Japanese cypress material of 50 mm width and 105 mm depth. The material length was 2000 mm. The plane used for measurements was a replaceable blade-type intermediate finish plane. The plane blade adjustment was left to the working subject. Table 1 presents characteristics of five skilled workers (group J) and 10 unskilled persons (group M). The author conducted motion analysis for them at a laboratory of Polytechnic University.

Group J in this study mainly comprises artisans who have won prizes in the Skill Grand Prix. All were first-class technicians. Skills Grand Prix is a tournament for those with level 1 technical skills, especially those with outstanding skills. Group M members were 10 unskilled people: 5 third-year students and 5 fourth-year students from a Japanese polytechnic university studying architecture in 2018.

TABLE I. Characteristics of Skilled and Unskilled Persons

No.	Height (cm)	Dominant hand	Dominant eye	Age	Carpentry experience (year)	Teaching history (year)	Remarks
J1	165	Right	Right	62	45	35	Skill Grand Prix 1st place
J2	165	Right	Right	72	55	40	Skill Grand Prix 1st place
J3	161	Right	Right	67	49	28	In-house training school instructor
J4	177	Right	Right	38	23	18	Skill Grand Prix 2nd place
J5	172	Right	Right	39	16	10	Certified training school instructor
M1	178	Right	Right	21	4	0	PTU, Arch, major 4th year
M2	177	Right	Right	22	4	0	PTU, Arch. major 4th year
M3	173	Right	Right	21	3	0	PTU, Arch. major 3rd year
M4	174	Right	Right	22	4	0	PTU, Arch. major 4th year
M5	165	Right	Right	21	3	0	PTU, Arch. major 3rd year
M6	180	Right	Right	20	3	0	PTU, Arch. major 3rd year
M7	170	Right	Right	21	3	0	PTU, Arch. major 3rd year
M8	168	Right	Right	20	3	0	PTU, Arch. major 3rd year
M9	178	Right	Right	22	4	0	PTU, Arch. major 4th year
M10	177	Right	Right	22	4	0	PTU, Arch. major 4th year

B. Preprocessing

We used software (MATLAB; The MathWorks Inc.) to analyze skeleton position data measured using Kinect™ at 0.03 s intervals. Table 2 presents data for one subject that were processed. Table 2 presents XYZ-axis values for 20 points of skeletal position data during planing work obtained from one shooting: the first column shows waist X axis data; the second shows waist Y axis data; and so on.

TABLE II. Data Example (Before Processing)

Time (s)	Waist X-axis (mm)	Waist Y-axis (mm)	Waist Z-axis (mm)	Spine X-axis (mm)	Spine Y-axis (mm)
0.03	-40.239	-762.46	1057.8	-37.527	-757.54
0.06	-40.121	-762.30	1057.8	-37.435	-757.48
0.09	-39.452	-760.96	1058.0	-36.798	-756.52
0.12	-37.735	-757.84	1057.9	-34.922	-753.77

Time (s)	Waist X-axis (mm)	Waist Y-axis (mm)	Waist Z-axis (mm)	Spine X-axis (mm)	Spine Y-axis (mm)
0.15	-35.893	-754.11	1058.5	-32.863	-750.72
0.18	-32.994	-750.87	1057.8	-29.517	-748.11
0.21	-29.873	-747.39	1056.8	-26.216	-745.33
0.24	-27.388	-743.58	1055.5	-23.721	-742.15
0.27	-25.869	-740.55	1055.5	-21.958	-739.66

Among the data for 20 points of skeletal position information in Table 2, skeleton position information of the head, shoulder, waist, and left hand, which has been emphasized in earlier studies, is the subject of analyses in this study. Using these data groups, the data were processed into a machine-learning format for analysis using the k-means method. Table 3 presents an example of a dataset obtained by processing information related to the head, shoulder, waist, and left hand for each subject.

TABLE III. DATA EXAMPLE (PROCESSING FOR CLUSTER ANALYSIS)

J1, 1st experiment, 2nd plane	J1, 1st experiment, 3rd plane	...	J1, 1st experiment, 7th plane	J1 2nd experiment, 2nd plane	...
-382.37	-410.78	...	-306.42	-352.84	...
-377.42	-399.05	...	-308.62	-357.03	...
-376.92	-396.86	...	-299.68	-357.81	...
-364.65	-394.47	...	-299.32	-356.31	...
-363.17	-389.36	...	-298.31	-349.42	...
-360.46	-385.36	...	-291.69	-328.33	...
-364.44	-369.31	...	-289.85	-333.24	...
-355.89	-364.90	...	-284.37	-337.13	...
-351.41	-348.89	...	-279.63	-334.60	...

Data in Table 2 include those of eight consecutive planing works. Therefore, the data in Table 3 are divided into those of six planing works excluding the first and last planing work pieces. The time-series data of the location information for each planing work of each subject are arranged in one column as one dataset. A dataset for each XYZ axis value comprises head, shoulder, waist, and left hand data. Therefore, 12 datasets are handled as one-dimensional data.

For preprocessing, data are standardized: the average of each column data becomes 0. The time series of the data were also checked: abnormal behaviors (values that should have increased had decreased, etc.) were excluded from time series data for the corresponding single-cutting operation.

The time required for a planing work piece differs every time. Therefore, the number of lines of motion data obtained in time-series differs for each planing work piece. Therefore, the number of rows in the dataset must be unified. Based on the planing operation with the longest planing work time, the blank after the other planing work was filled entirely with zeros.

C. *Analytical method*

Collecting large amounts of data has become easier because of improvements in computer processing speed and communication infrastructure. Furthermore, big data are analyzed and used in various fields. Performing this big data analysis manually would be very expensive and impractical. For this reason, machine learning, which can automatically obtain accurate results from large amounts of data in a shorter time than humans could reasonably achieve, is often used. Machine learning can resolve difficulties by inferring patterns from large amounts of data. Therefore, for this study, we decided to conduct analyses using the K-means algorithm, a method of unsupervised learning, as the first experiment to explore training effects using machine learning in the vocational training field. There are two reasons that the k-means method was chosen as the machine learning technique. The first being simple clustering technique. The second is to explain many data in a short time. The author chose it because this k-means method meets both requirements for the purpose of this article.

Equation (1) presents evaluation function f of the k-means algorithm. Data X are divided into arbitrary K clusters by finding the center of the cluster that minimizes Equation (1).

$$f = \sum_{X_j \in X} \min_{i \in X} \|X_j - c_i\| \quad (1)$$

Where X_j, $j \in \{1,\ldots,n\}$ represents each datum; n denotes the total number of data. Also, c_i signifies the cluster center i^j $n\{1,\ldots,k\}$. The k-means method performs clustering by obtaining a cluster center that minimizes the distance between each data point and the nearest cluster center.

IV. EXPERIMENTS

As described herein, we try to discriminate between movements of skilled and untrained persons based on acquisition of motion data. In doing so, we aim to clarify unique behaviors that are typical of skilled workers.

A. *Preliminary analysis*

First, cluster analysis was applied to divide the data into two by k-means using 12 datasets of XYZ axes of the head, shoulder, waist, and left hand shown in Section III.B as one matrix. A value of k was chosen as 2 is because it confirms the usefulness of the k-means method. In addition, one can see if clustering can be categorized broadly into skilled and unskilled people. The reason for choosing the head, shoulder, waist, and left hand is that they were also chosen in earlier studies [5]. One can ascertain the characteristics of the posture of the subject with planing work. Results show simple classification according to the length of time needed for the work. Work speed is an effective index for evaluating work movements, but specific movements common to skilled workers have not been clarified. Therefore, to exclude information related to work speed and to compare detailed movements in the planing work of the respective subjects, results demonstrated the necessity of conducting analyses using positional information aligned within a certain time interval.

B. Experiment method

This study specifically examines movements in the first few seconds of planing work and during the first few seconds before the end of the movement. Specifically examining the start and end of planing, they have their own movements. Therefore, the skill levels are easier to understand than during planing. To organize the time-series data of the obtained motion, the interval from the start to 2.25 s (initial interval) and the interval from 2.25 s before the end to the end time (final interval) were set. The reason to set the time to 2.25 s is the necessary amount of data to identify work trends. Then, the 75 time-series position information data included in each section were made into one matrix. The data were divided into two clusters using k-means.

C. Experiment results for interval

The experimentally obtained results for the initial interval presented in section IV.B are described in IV.C.1). Experimentally obtained results for the final interval are described in IV.C.2).

1) Experiment results of the initial interval

The analysis specifically examined movement for 2.25 s from the start of movement. Data were divided into two by k-means for a matrix containing all data in the X-axis, Y-axis, and Z-axis directions (including the head, shoulder, waist, and left hand). Results show rough classification by skilled and unskilled persons. Figure 4 presents classification results for each planing work by skilled and unskilled workers obtained using location information in the initial interval.

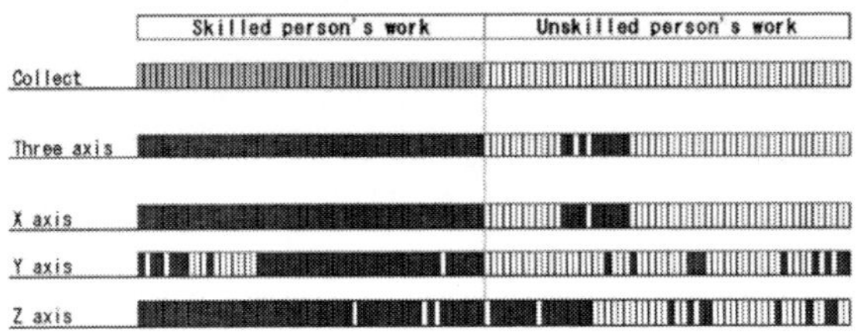

Figure 4. Results of clustering by skeletal position in the initial interval.

In addition, to ascertain which of the three directions is most effective for clustering, we divided the datasets in the X-axis, Y-axis, and Z-axis directions and applied cluster analysis using each dataset to ascertain key factors for classification. As shown in Figure 4, results show that the movement in the X-axis direction had an effect. Therefore, the head, shoulder, waist, and left hand were clustered into two clusters using the k-means method to find out which part of the X-axis movement most affected clustering. As shown in Figure 5, all factors affecting the head, shoulder, waist, and left hand were confirmed as influential.

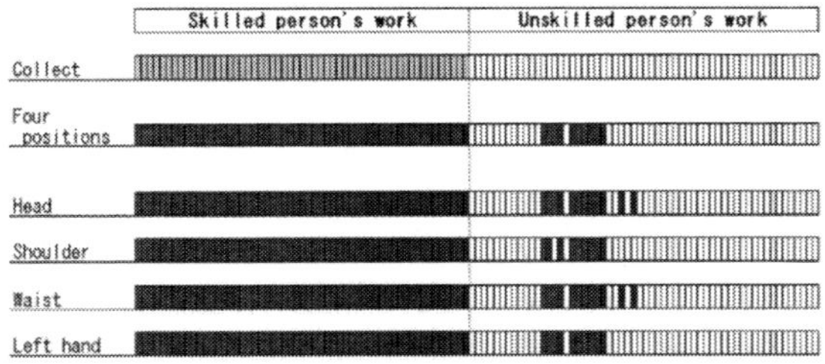

Figure 5. Results of clustering by skeletal position in the X-axis direction at the initial interval.

2) Experiment result of the final interval

These analyses specifically addressed the period of 2.25 s of movement until the end of movement. Data were divided into two parts using k-means for a matrix containing all data in the X-axis, Y-axis, and Z-axis directions (including the head, shoulder, waist, and left hand). As described in IV.C.1), results show rough classification of skilled and untrained work. Figure 6 shows how planing work by a skilled person and by an unskilled person is classifiable using position information in the final interval.

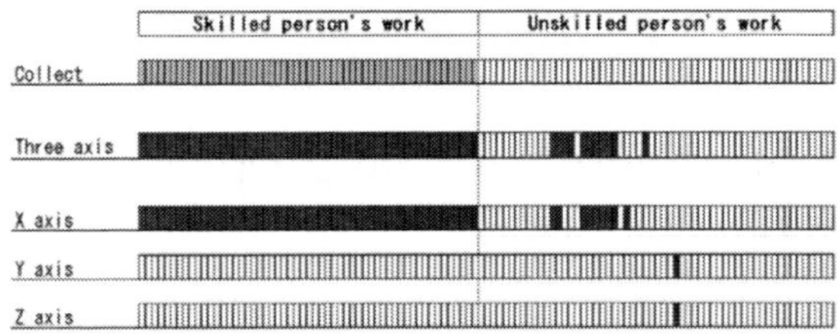

Figure 6. Results of clustering by skeletal position in the final interval.

In addition, to ascertain which of the three directions is most effective for clustering, after dividing the datasets in the X-axis, Y-axis, and Z-axis directions to ascertain key factors for classification, we applied cluster analysis using each dataset. Figure 7 presents experimentally obtained results for X. As in IV.C.1), results demonstrated that movement in the X-axis direction was affected. Therefore, the head, shoulder, waist, and left hand were clustered into two clusters by the k-means method to ascertain which part of the X-axis movement most affected clustering. On the X-axis, all head, shoulder, waist, and left hand effects were confirmed.

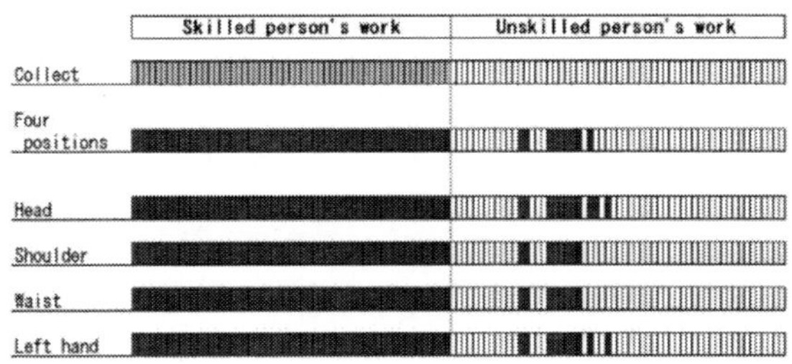

Figure 7. Results of clustering by skeletal position in the X-axis direction at the final interval.

Results presented above show that a feature exists in movement in the X-axis direction in the initial interval and final interval. To examine the factors that led to this analysis, we examined the video during the experiment and the raw data of the head, shoulder, waist, and left hand. Furthermore, all elements of the head, shoulder, waist, and left hand are affected. This effect might be attributable to the number of pauses used by skilled and unskilled persons during one bout of planing work. Skilled persons use a large forward-leaning posture because the pauses during planing work are few: 0–2 times. This tendency was also observed for unskilled workers clustered in the same group as skilled workers. However, unskilled workers in different groups tend to use a slightly forward-leaning posture because they pause several times (1–6 times) during planing work. Therefore, cluster analysis revealed differences between efficient work with few stops and work with numerous stops.

V. CONCLUSION

The purpose of this study was to construct a system to analyze and visualize big data related to training that can be acquired during vocational training. Then we conducted experiments to evaluate planing work to improve training efficiency, and found the possibility. The experiments specifically examined the initial interval and final interval, and included application of cluster analysis using k-means with position information obtained for four skeletal locations: the head, shoulder, waist, and left hand. Results show clustering of results by skilled and unskilled people. These results confirmed that applying simple machine learning such as k-means to planing work training data can engender useful analysis. This study used only four skeleton positions for analytical information. For that reason, only analysis that is related closely to the number of stops during planing is possible. In the past, analyses that were performed manually could be performed quickly using machine learning. The present study assessed clusters of skilled and unskilled people. Future studies, by performing clustering among unskilled people, are expected to provide optimal skill instruction for individual groups. Therefore, in this paper, we were able to analyze only the number of stops during planing. Future studies will use analytical methods to generate posture data from the measured three-axis data assess methods to analyze data for the load applied to the work material during planing work operations. Promoting this research can improve training effects in the field of vocational training by producing a continuous support system using machine learning.

ACKNOWLEDGMENTS

This work was supported by JSPS KAKENHI Grants No. 18K13254, 16K00157, 26350221, 15H02920, and 19K15248.

Figures 1 and 2 were from Professor Emeritus Shinichiro Matsudome of the Polytechnic University. The author acknowledges that contribution and appreciates it earnestly.

REFERENCES

[1] Ministry of Land, Infrastructure, Transport and Tourism Construction statistics survey report, total for 2018. [Online]. Available from: http://www.mlit.go.jp/sogoseisaku/jouhouka/sosei_jouhouka_tk4_000002.html/ [retrieved: 12,2019]

[2] Statistics Bureau, Ministry of Internal Affairs and Communications. Census 1971: Extraction details National result table number 18. [Online]. Available from: https://www.e-stat.go.jp/stat-search/files?page=1&layout=datalist&toukei=00200521&bunya_l=02&tstat=000001037125&cycle=0&tclass1=000001037140&stat_infid=000007915263&result_page=1&second=1&second2=1/ [retrieved: 12,2019]

[3] Statistics Bureau, Ministry of Internal Affairs and Communications. Census 2015: Extraction details National result table number 9. [Online]. Available from: https://www.e-stat.go.jp/stat-search/files?page=1&layout=datalist&toukei=00200521&tstat=000001080615&cycle=0&tclass1=000001104855&tclass2=000001108965&stat_infid=000031643878&cycle_facet=tclass1%3Acycle&second2=1/ [retrieved: 12,2019]

[4] H. Tsukazaki, M. Tamai, K. Kondo, H. Maekawa, and S. Matsudome, "A study on the behavior analysis of carpenter skills." Summaries of Technical Papers of Annual Meeting. Architectural Institute of Japan, pp.59-60, 2016.

[5] H. Kataoka, H. Tsukazaki, M. Sadanari, H. Maekawa, T. Sahata, K. Nishiguchi et al. "A study of the behavior analysis of carpenter skills – Instruction method of planing work." Summaries of Technical Papers of Annual Meeting. Architectural Institute of Japan, pp.147-148, 2019.

[6] G. Chen, A. Yamashita, K. Shibaki, and C. Tanaka, "Three-dimensional analyses of the work motion using woodworking tools I: Basic from of planing motion of skilled Japanese woodworkers." Mokuzai Gakkaishi Vol.48, No.2, The Japan Wood Research Society, pp.80-88, 2002.

[7] G. Chen, A. Yamashita, K. Shibaki, and C. Tanaka, "Three-dimensional analysis of the work motion using woodworking tools II: Comparison on the sawing motions of the skilled and no-skilled woodworker." Mokuzai Gakkaishi Vol.49, No.3, The Japan Wood Research Society, pp.171-178, 2003.

[8] S. Kurebayashi, K. Kobayashi, D. Takayama, K. Eguchi, and S. Kanemune, "The Development of Basic Motion-Analysis Using the Sensor KINECT." Bulletin of the Japan Society of Industrial and Technical Education Vol.55, No.3, pp.213-220, 2013.

[9] H. Ishikawa, Social Big Data Mining. CRC Press, March 2015.

A New Advertisement Method of Displaying a Crowd

Taku Watanabe
Department of Computer Science and Engineering
Waseda University, Japan
e-mail: t.watanabe@dcl.cs.waseda.ac.jp

Yuta Matsushima
Department of Computer Science and Engineering,
Waseda University, Japan
e-mail: y.matsushima@dcl.cs.waseda.ac.jp

Kenji Tsukamoto
Department of Computer Science and Engineering,
Waseda University, Japan
e-mail: tenbook223@dcl.cs.waseda.ac.jp

Kota Gushima
Department of Computer Science and Engineering,
Waseda University, Japan
e-mail: gushi@dcl.cs.waseda.ac.jp

Tatsuo Nakajima
Department of Computer Scient and Engineering
Waseda University, Japan
e-mail: tatsuo@dcl.cs.waseda.ac.jp

***Abstract*—In this paper, using a new advertising method within a virtual space, we examine a method that portrays a crowd by showing multiple people in front of institutions and stores. This method is intended to promote advertising by utilizing the behavioral psychology of users who want to agree with what many other people support. We examine how the attractiveness of the store changes due to the presence or absence of crowds in a shopping mall within a virtual space. Although there were some subjects whose store ratings were not increased due to the negative image of crowds and the unnaturalness of the crowds, the proposed method generally increased the appeal of the store and the subjects' impression of the store.**

Keywords-Virtual Reality; Bandwagon Effect.

I. INTRODUCTION

In recent years, with the development of virtual reality technologies, there have been many attempts to represent actual facilities, services, stores, etc. in virtual spaces [1]-[3]. Attempts have been made to develop a virtual space as a social infrastructure and expand it as a place for people's activities [4]-[6]. As a result of such research, if virtual reality as a social infrastructure expands in the future and becomes the basis of human activities, users will be able to perform more free-of-charge activities in the virtual world than they can in the real world. Currently, while attempts are being made to communicate information to users via various forms of media [7], it is noteworthy that when advertising activities are conducted in a virtual society, this method of expression spreads information more than when using conventional methods. For example, while disseminating information throughout a shopping mall or department store is possible in a virtual world, methods of poster text, illustrations, and voice guidance must generally be used in the real world. On the other hand, objects existing in the virtual world can be converted and alternatively expressed by using information technologies, and a more flexible transmission method can be expected. In this paper, we propose a method of displaying crowds as a way to guide users. The purpose of the method is to portray a thriving situation by placing multiple virtual people in front of the store, event, or object that the system wants to advertise, as shown in Figure 1. It is hypothesized that this approach makes it possible to advertise in a way that is more suitable to the situation than is the traditional text-based guidance.

Figure 1. Displaying a Crowd.

The rest of the paper proceeds as follows: Section 2 describes the background of this study. In Section 3, we explain the concepts of new advertisement method of displaying a crowd and an experiment to verify the effect of displaying crowd. The result of this experiments is presented in Section 4. In Section 5, we discuss the obtained results after the experiment. Finally, Section 6 concludes this paper.

II. BACKGROUND

This section introduces the background that led to the proposal of our advertising method.

A. Bandwagon Effect and Snob Effect

The concept behind this advertising effect approach is the bandwagon effect that exists in human behavioral psychology [8]. The bandwagon effect is a psychological phenomenon in which people think that something that many other people support is valuable. This effect is used in economic marketing and can be incorporated into advertising effects that sell products to customers [9][10]. Political studies have suggested a relationship with the voter rate of elections [11]-[14]. On the other hand, there is also a psychological phenomenon where people want to keep their perception of scarcity and do not want to own what many people support. This is called the snob effect or the underdog effect. These effects are not contradictory but rooted in human behavioral psychology [15][16].

B. Introducing the Bandwagon Effect based on IoT Technologies

Research is being conducted to investigate the impact of introducing this bandwagon effect to IoT-based systems. In the study of [17], a recommended system incorporating the bandwagon effect is considered from the user's selection history. In recent years, a system that the user operates digitally and without thinking has become popular. This experiment is one example of the research that is related to persuasion without attracting the user's attention [18]. In addition, by adopting the method of giving only the necessary information to the user of a digital device, the user can select their level of necessary information according to the environment of their future society in which the amount of information increases enormously [19]. In the study of [20], the authors proposed solutions to public institution bottlenecks by providing information about the surrounding environment and presenting it to the user. As described above, such research has been conducted to enrich people's lives by providing information on the everyday world in which people live.

III. A PROPOSED APPROACH AND ITS EXPERIMENT DESIGN

As an approach to inducing people, it is effective to examine human psychology, and such methods are currently being studied [21]. In this paper, we propose an advertising method of portraying a shop as being one that many people support as a way to guide the target shops. Specifically, a crowd is displayed in front of a store as an expression that it is supported by many people in a virtual space, as shown in Figures 2-4. By using the projection method that places virtual people in stores within a virtual shopping mall, the natural guidance that makes users feel as comfortable as possible is realized. In this case, the method may be effective for users who are strongly oriented to joining bandwagons, as it emphasizes the support of the majority. In addition, it is necessary to consider how to respond when the same approach is attempted on user who is highly snob-effect oriented.

In the remaining section, we show how the experiment investigating the effectiveness of our approach is designed.

A. Preliminary Survey

Before starting the experiments, we examine the psychological tendencies of subjects in their daily life. This is because the results will vary greatly depending on whether their human behavioral psychological intention to follow a large number of opinions (bandwagonism) or their desire to retain one's rarity (snobbish) is stronger. In the preliminary survey as shown in TABLE I, several questions regarding the subject's bandwagonism are prepared in the form of a 6-point Likert score. We classify people who responded positively to a large number of opinion-based answers with an average score of 3.5 or higher as a "Bandwagoner", and those who scored less than that value are classified as a "Snob".

TABLE I. THE CONTENTS OF PRELIMINARY SURVEYS

No	Question
Q1	*Do you decide your actions by looking at the people around you?*
Q2	*Would you like to go to a store recommended on TV or the web?*
Q3	*Would you like to go to a shop that has gained a reputation from word of mouth?*
Q4	*What kind of shop do you care about when you find thriving shops on the street?*
Q5	*Are you interested in shops that are said to be in line with other people?*

B. Patrolling in the Virtual Mall

After the preliminary survey is completed, the subject conducts a patrol through the virtual shopping mall with the headset attached as shown in Figure 5. Three clothing stores in the mall are set as destinations, the presence or absence of a crowd is compared among the stores, and how the attraction level of the store changes depending on the crowd is evaluated on a 6-point Likert scale.

C. Post-Experimental Survey and Interview

After the patrol of the mall, we ask the subjects about the crowd conditions. Specifically, we ask, "*At what crowd level do you feel the charm of the store?*" and "*At what crowd level do you want to enter the store?*" The responses to these questions can either be "*Quiet*", "*Congested*", or "*Very Congested*". Furthermore, the model that expresses the crowd itself, the location where the crowd is generated, and whether the behavior of the model feels uncomfortable are all evaluated in 6 stages.

Not Crowded

Crowded

Figure 2. First Situation in a Virtual Mall.

Not Crowded

Crowded

Figure 3. Second Situation in a Virtual Mall.

Not Crowded

Crowded

Figure 4. Third Situation in a Virtual Mall.

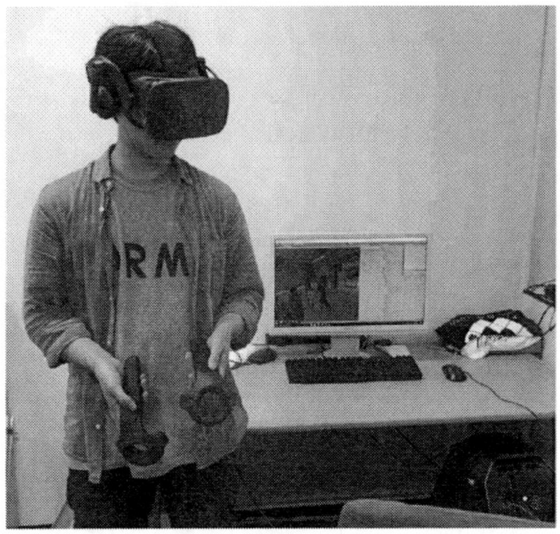

Figure 5. A Scene of Patrolling in a Virtual Mall.

TABLE II. DETAIL OF POST-EXPERIMENTAL INTERVIEWS

No	Question
Q1	Evaluation of Crowds as Advertisement
Q2	Discomfort with Human Models and Crowds
Q3	Facilities that May be Judged from Crowds

After all the experiments were completed, the subjects are interviewed from three viewpoints, as shown in TABLE II, to obtain their impressions and opinions on the crowd-controlled advertising.

IV. Results from the Experiment

The experiment described in Section 4 was conducted on 8 men and 1 woman. Based on the preliminary survey, those are were classified as a bandwagoner are expressed as B1, B2, …, and those who were classified as a snob are expressed as S1, S2, ….

A. Reactions from Patrolling the Virtual Mall

From the mall patrol experiment, it can be seen that although there is a difference in degree, the main intention is whether the person enters the store or not. Figure 6 shows the difference of score of stores' attractiveness by displaying crowd or not. Furthermore, the distributions of answers to the question related to displaying crowd are shown in Figure 7, 8.

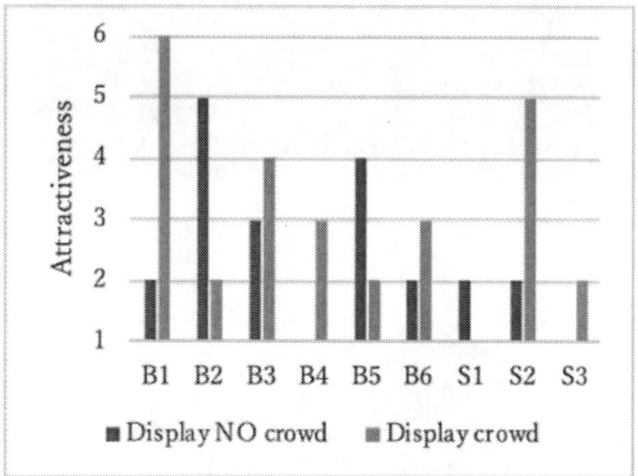

Figure 6. The Score of Store Impressions

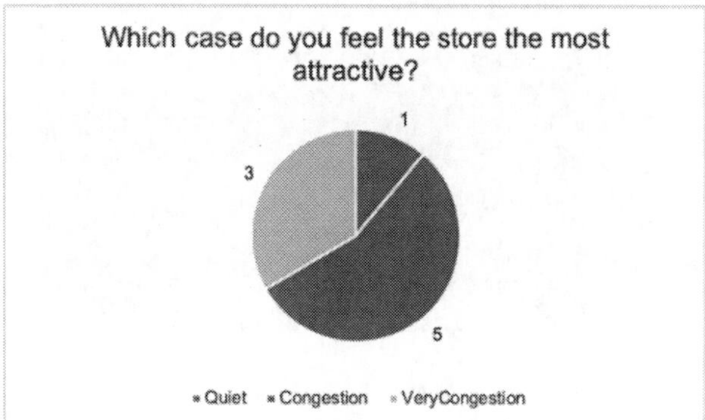

Figure 7. The Distribution of Answers to the question of how crowded

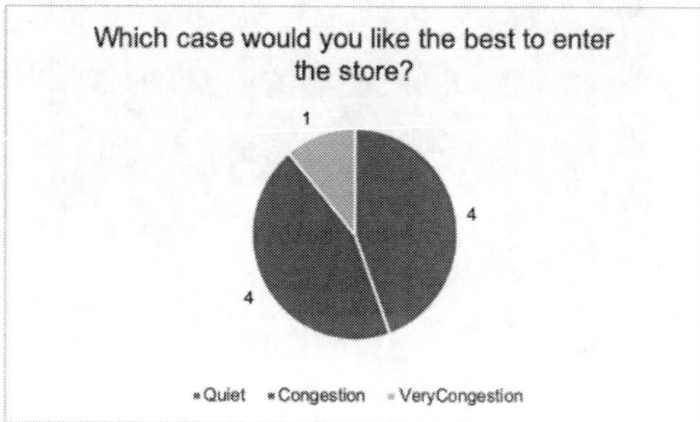

Figure 8. The Score of Stores Impression

B. Discomfort with Crowded Displays

Evaluating discomfort with crowded display methods shows that most users say that they feel uncomfortable with the projection, as shown in Figure 9.

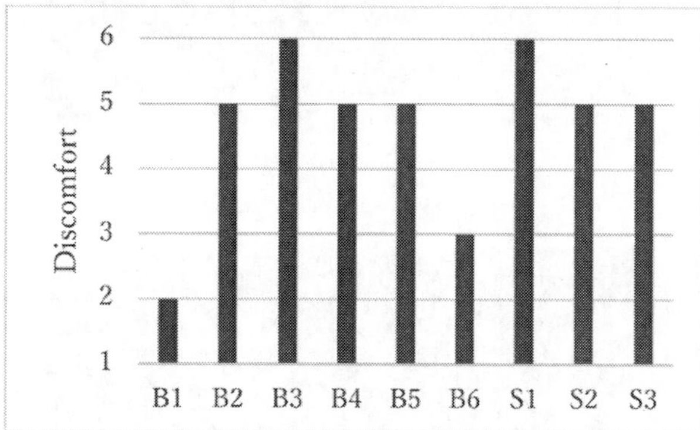

Figure 9. The Score of Discomfort of Human Models

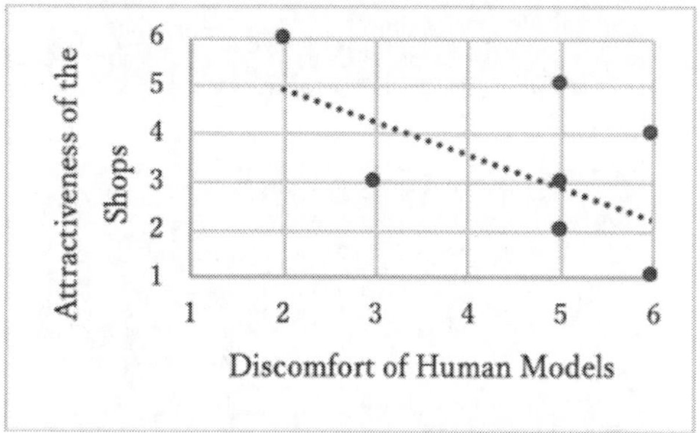

Figure 10. The Score of Store Impressions

Furthermore, as a result of calculating the correlation between the evaluation of an uncomfortable feeling with respect to the crowd and the evaluation of the crowd display from the scatter diagram of Figure 10, the correlation coefficient was calculated to be approximately −0.57.

V. Discussions

In this section, we examine whether our proposed method has the potential to be used as an advertising technique based on the results of the experiments.

A. Feasibility of the Bandwagon Approach

First, the experiments and surveys suggested that the presence of people in a store was a factor in the overall appeal of the store itself and that this tendency existed regardless of whether the shopper was a bandwagoner or a snob. It can be considered that a sense of security was obtained when people were shown that the store was supported by way of the presence of a crowd in the store. In addition, the subjects answered in the interview that "*I want to go to this store when it is available* (S2)" or "*I want to check out this store when I return* (B3)".

Even if there was no immediate effect of crowding as a form of advertisement, it can be considered that this approach does leave an impression on the user. In addition, there was an opinion that the approach of displaying crowds is reliable and interesting because it suggests a guarantee that the store is popular at that moment compared to Internet reviews and conventional advertisements (S2). On the other hand, there were both bandwagoner and snob subjects who replied that the appeal of the store decreased with respect to the crowd display (B2, B5, S1). It was noted that the evaluation values change depending on the negative impression of the crowd itself and the type of store that advertises using a crowd. Furthermore, the display of a crowd may interfere with the appearance of the store. In such cases, the store may not be able to showcase the information that it truly wants to show to customers, such as store design, recommended products, discount advertisements, etc.

B. Current Problems of the Proposed Method

A couple of subjects expressed the opinion that there were problems with the proposed method (B2, B4). In addition, it was mentioned that the model as adverse effects, such as imparting too much stress on the user and making it difficult to enter the store because too many people were standing in the entrance (B4, B6, S1). Therefore, it is thought that the size of the crowd must be adjusted within a range that does not disturb the scenery of the store.

The most prevalent opinion expressed in this experiment was that the subject felt uncomfortable in the situation where people were crowded in front of the store (B1, B2, B4, B5, B6, S1, S3). In reality, the situation in which people are crowded in front of the store is unnatural; therefore, some subjects said they felt anxiety that an incident had occurred in the store (B6) or it was a problematic store (S1).

Furthermore, the appropriateness of the store displaying a crowd is related to the uncomfortable feeling produced by such a crowd. In this situation, the subject was supposed to go to a clothing store, but at the clothing store, the subject said that congestion at the store was not preferable for reasons, such as wanting to talk to a store clerk or try on clothing (B2).

Therefore, it is desirable that the facilities and stores that display crowds guarantee their value due to the presence of additional people, e.g., restaurants that require up-to-date evaluations (B6, S2), movie theaters in which the state of the facilities cannot be seen from outside (B4), live events that are increased by crowds (S1), and station congestion information disseminated through the display of crowds (S3). As shown in Figure 10, the uncomfortable feeling related to crowding has a negative correlation with the attractiveness of the store; therefore, reducing the uncomfortable feeling of crowding will be a future challenge.

C. Concern About Using the System in the Real World

In this paper, we proposed a method to display crowds as a form of advertisement. It is thought that the advertising effect of displaying crowds can be expected to some extent in the virtual world, but there are various concerns about using this method in the real world.

The first concern is that it must be possible to distinguish the objects that are projected to the user while also harmonizing with the existing objects (B4). This is because if the user cannot actually distinguish between displayed and real objects when walking around the city or facilities, there will be problems, such as collision with surrounding people and forcing the user to perform useless actions, such as avoiding the projected objects. However, as described above, there is the problem of the advertising effect being slim unless the user can be guided without a sense of incongruity. To implement this advertising method in reality, it is necessary to consider a good projection method that resolves these conflicts. In interviews with the subjects, model methods were suggested that both avoid the user (B4) and that display the crowd only at a distance and disappear when the user moves close to the crowd (S2). It is necessary to further verify how the advertising effect will change by introducing these methods.

The second concern is that the approach could be used for so-called stealth marketing, in which the store intentionally manipulates the crowd to enforce the store's advertisements without notice to the user, and thus the user cannot make the correct choice (B6). We must be careful of the social problems caused by malicious stealth marketing [22]

VI. Conclusion And Future Work

The possibility of a new advertising method in the virtual world was considered through the current experiment. This method cannot be applied to every facility or store, but it can be used to relate the prosperity and reputation of a store at a glance and to attract people's attention. This approach can be used for a facility that is directly related to popularity, such as a restaurant, or an event that gathers people with the same purpose, such as a live performance.

In the next step of our research, we will verify whether it is possible to reduce the user's uncomfortable feeling toward the crowd displayed in the shopping mall by changing the location, the viewing location, the number of people, and the behavior of the crowd. We will also evaluate how the attractiveness of the store changes as the feeling of discomfort decreases. In addition, it is considered necessary to verify how the user's impression of the store changes by changing the type of store that displays crowds in front of them.

Furthermore, through interviews, we will evaluate whether the risk of actually using the system in reality can be reduced by introducing a method to lower the risk of using the technique. It is thought that it is necessary to verify and evaluate how discomfort with the crowd changes by introducing this method and whether the projection has an advertising effect.

REFERENCES

[1] M. Speicher, S. Cucerca, and A. Krüger, "VRShop: A Mobile Interactive Virtual Reality Shopping Environment Combining the Benefits of On- and Offline Shopping", Proceedings of the ACM on Interactive, Mobile, Wearable and Ubiquitous Technologies, Volume 1 Issue 3, September 2017, Article No. 102, [online] Available from: https://doi.org/10.1145/3130967, accessed 2020/01/02

[2] K. Oiwake, K. Komiya, H. Akasaki, and T. Nakajima, "VR Classroom: Enhancing Learning Experience with Virtual Class Rooms", 2018, pp.1-6

[3] H. Tsuboi, S. Toyama, and T. Nakajima, "Enhancing Bicycle Safety Through Immersive Experiences Using Virtual Reality Technologies". International Conference on Augmented Cognition 2018, pp.444-456

[4] D. P. Brutzman, M. R. Macedonia, and M. J. Zyda, "Internetwork Infrastructure Requirements for Virtual Environment", The unpredictable Certainly: White Papers, pp.110-122, 2000,

[5] T. L. Taylor, "Life in Virtual Worlds: Plural Existence, Multimodalities, and Other Online Research Challenges.", American Behavioral Scientist 43, no.3, November 1999 pp.436–449

[6] M. N. Boulos, L. Hetherington and S. Wheeler, "Second Life: an overview of the potential of 3-D virtual worlds in medical and health education", Health Information and Libraries Journal, Volume 24, Issue 4, December 2007, pp.233-308,

[7] A. Shankar and B. Horton, "Ambient media: advertising's new media opportunity?", International Journal of Advertising, The Review of Marketing Communications, March 02 2015, pp.305-321.

[8] H. Leibenstein, "Bandwagon, Snob and Veblen Effects in the Theory of Consumers' Demand", The Quarterly Journal of Economics, May 1950, pp.183-207

[9] N. McBride, "Business use of the internet: Strategic decision or another bandwagon?", European Management Journal, Volume 15, Issue 1, February 1997, pp.58-67

[10] P. Nitin and S. Klein, "Bandwagon Pressures and Interfirm Alliances in the Global Pharmaceutical Industry."Journal of International Marketing, vol. 6, No. 2, June 1998, pp.54–73

[11] H. A. Simon, "Bandwagon and Underdog Effects and the Possibility of Election Predictions", Public Opinion Quarterly, Volume 18, Issue 3, FALL 1954, pp.245–253

[12] I. McAllister and D. T. Studlar, "Bandwagon, Underdog, or Projection? Opinion Polls and Electoral Choice in Britain, 1979-1987", The Journal of Politics 1991 53:3, pp.720-741

[13] C. E. Zech, "Leibenstein's bandwagon effect as applied to Voting", Public Choice, Volume 21, Issue 1, pp.117-122, March 1975

[14] R. Schmitt-Beck, "Mass Media, the Electorate, and the Bandwagon. a Study of Communication Effects on Vote Choice in Germany", International Journal of Public Opinion Research, Volume 8, Issue 3, FALL 1996, pp.266–291

[15] Y. Aragaki et al., "Bandwagon effect and snob effect that occur within the same consumer.",Chuo University Faculty of Commerse, 2012, [online] Avaiable from: http://c-faculty.chuo-u.ac.jp/~shoyuki/2012%20bandwagon%20and%20snob.pdf, accessed 2019/10/05

[16] Y. Kuwashima, "Structural Equivalence and Cohesion Can Explain Bandwagon and Snob Effect", Annals of Business Administrative Science, 2016, Volume 15, Issue 1, pp.1-14

[17] S. Choi, H. Lee, Y. Han, K. L. Man, and W. K. Chong, "A Recommendation Model Using the Bandwagon Effect for E-Marketing Purposes in IoT." International Journal of Distributed Sensor Networks, July 7, 2015, [online] Available from: https://journals.sagepub.com/doi/10.1155/2015/475163, accessed 2020/01/02

[18] J. Ham, C. Midden, and F. Beute, "Can ambient persuasive technology persuade unconsciously?: using subliminal feedback to influence energy consumption ratings of household appliances", Persuasive '09, April 2009, Article No.29, pp.1-6

[19] K. Gushima, H. Akasaki, and T. Nakajima, "Ambient bot: delivering daily casual information through eye contact with an intimate virtual creature", AcademicMindtrek '17, September 20-21, 2017, pp.231-234

[20] G. Boehm, "Ambient Persuasive Guidance", TEI '11, January 2011, pp.431-432

[21] J. M. Weyant, "Applying Social Psychology to Induce Charitable Donations", Journal of Applied Social Psychology banner, Volume14, Issue5, October 1984, pp.441-447

[22] K. D. Martin and N. C. Smith, "Commercializing Social Interaction: The Ethics of Stealth Marketing", INSEAD Business School Research Paper No.2008/19/ISIC, March 2008, pp.1-36.

AiArt: Towards Artificial Intelligence Art

Weiwen Chen
Academy of Arts and Design
Tsinghua University
Beijing, China
Email: cww-lisa@outlook.com

Mohammad Shidujaman
Academy of Arts and Design
Tsinghua University
Beijing, China
Email: shangt15@mails.tsinghua.edu.cn

Xuelin Tang
Academy of Arts and Design
Tsinghua University
Beijing, China
Email: m18273126206@163.com

Abstract— **With the advance of Artificial Intelligence (AI) applied profoundly into different areas of industries, a growing number of artists have shown great interest in exploring and discovering the potential possibilities of AI in art through embracing the latest techniques, such as neural networks and deep learning. As a result, a new kind of art named artificial intelligence art (AiArt) has emerged, which is a creative activity that combines artists with technical experts, intelligent robots, and audience by using AI as the core medium to create, express thoughts and emotions. The purpose of this article is to define the AiArt as an approach to distinguish it from other art forms and provide new inspiration and direction for art practitioners, theoreticians and scientists, which is related to one of the topics of the conference like "artificial intelligence injected artistic creation". This paper first briefly reviews the recent development of AiArt and then attempts a discussion about the essence and characteristics of this new form of art through analyzing the disciplines behind the AI artworks. Finally, this paper draws the conclusion that the diversification of subjects, the intelligence of the media, and the modernization of expression are the nature of AiArt, which are the fundamental signs that distinguish AiArt from traditional arts, such as painting, sculpture, and digital art. In addition to the creative, historical, and aesthetic characteristics of general art, we suppose there are more four new features in AiArt: synesthesia experience, flowability and changeability, interaction and communication, and penetration and integration.**

Keywords-artificial intelligence (AI); art; artificial intelligence art (AiArt); AiArt essence; AiArt characteristics.

I. INTRODUCTION

It is a truth universally acknowledged that art always has a long-standing, complex and continually evolving relationship with science and technology. As with advanced technologies, some artists will gradually abandon the previous tools they used to create artworks and attempt to utilize the newest inventions as an alternative medium, which has huge impacts on art that is produced, and the way art is perceived and apprehended by viewers [1]. Like the invention of pigments, the printing press, photography and computers, it is believed that AI is a new revolution of technology that will radically alter the way people make artworks and extend our creative potential and imagination [2].

AI is a domain of computer science whose purpose is to explore the limits and the methods of using digital computers to simulate [3][4], extend and expand functions carried out by the human brains, such as obtaining and dealing information through the senses, understanding natural languages and solving a complex problem [5]. Over the past 20 years, with the support of big data and cloud computing, AI has made breakthroughs in key technologies, such as machine learning, natural language processing, speech recognition and computer vision. In this context, more and more artists have keenly captured the applicational prospects of AI technology in the art field [6], and been eager to use AI media to carry out artistic creation without hesitation. Hence, the combination of AI and art has given birth to a new form of art called AiArt, which has its own unique artistic standards and features that need us to research and redefine.

At the same time, theoretical researches on AiArt are far left behind its practices. It is rare that there are few types of research focusing on the ideological and theoretical level of AiArt, but most of the papers are written from the perspective of technique and application. In 1983, a digital artist named Stephen Wilson [7] put forward an anticipation of the future trend for computer art that developments in AI might make artworks created by artists learn from experience and interact with audiences in intelligent ways with human-like sensibilities, and stressed the importance of AI to visual artists who are encouraged to participate in this inevitable trend. Kaifu Li, an AI expert, published a monograph called Artificial Intelligence in 2017, which has discussed the relationship between AI and artistic creation [8]. He believed the artistic process based on AI algorithms is only the simple imitation of a particular creative style of artworks created by artists through learning a lot of human works as a database. Thus, there is no possibility that computers are able to approach or surpass human artists in the next few years. Liqing Tan, a famous artist, has given a bold interpretation and prediction for the development of AiArt in the future and put forward the concept of singularity art [9]. He has discussed the challenges that artists will face when it comes to strong AI and analyzed the nature and characteristics of singularity art and the new type of relationship between artists and the audience. He supposed that singularity art is a high combination of human intelligence and AI when science and technology reach the singularity. Singularity artists are no longer just creators and messengers, but participants and coordinators; experiencers are no longer just external watchers, but also participants and creators. There is no clear distinction between viewers and creators. Some scholars thought that AiArt is more intelligent and autonomous which make them separate from traditional computer art and it can help to improve the imagination, creativity, perception that computer did not have before [10]. In short, theoretical researches on AiArt which is neither comprehensively nor deeply, has just begun, and requires vigorous improvement and development.

It is generally thought that the practice of AI, which artists use as core medium to create a growing number of intelligent artworks has flourished, and the birth of enthralling artistic robots has shown the fabulous and outstanding ability of imitation [11]. However, what exactly is the AiArt? What is the nature and characteristics of AiArt? What are the principles and prospects of AiArt? Those are the questions that need to be answered urgently from the theoretical aspect with the gradual exploration into AiArt, otherwise, the AiArt practice will develop blindly. Therefore, this article aims to answer the question of what AiArt is theoretically, that is, to find out the essence of AiArt as new features that make it different from other forms of art.

In Section 2, we review briefly AI artworks with the development of science and technology.. In Section 3, we discuss the essence of AiArt. In Section 4, we conclude the characteristics of AiArt. It would be a better understanding of this new type of art, the importance of combining computers and humans, and the new relationship between AI, artists, art robots, and audiences.

II. A BRIEF REVIEW ON THE DEVELOPMENT OF AIART

The AiArt has an ongoing and long-standing relationship with the advance of AI technology. The development of AiArt, therefore, has gone through three stages: germination stage, rising stage and popularization stage. Figure 1 explains the three stages of the development of AiArt.

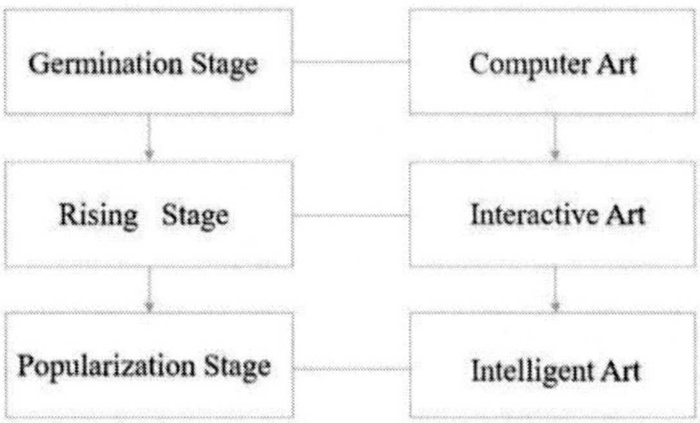

Figure 1. Three stages of the development of AiArt

A. The first stage

From the 1960s to the end of the 20th century is the embryonic stage of AiArt, that is, the stage of computer art. AI is a domain of computer science, thus computer art is the forerunner and foundation of AiArt. At this stage, some foreign artists and art writers have begun to generate artworks enthusiastically with the aid of digital computer programs. They need to conceive the visual art patterns they want in their minds from the start, and then write the corresponding program code to achieve the desired renderings and drawings of mathematical features. At the beginning of 1960, Desmond Hen, a lecturer at the University of Manchester, used the bomb simulation computer program used in World War II to continuously manufacture the world's earliest automatic drawing machines named the Henry drawing machine [12]. In 1963, the American computer magazine "Computer and Automation" organized the first computer image competition, which ignited the craze for computer image creation. Harold Cohen, an art professor at the University of California, San Diego, is one of the earliest explorers of computer art. He wrote the AARON computer program to create a series of regular images [13]. Figure 2 shows the process of creating artwork by AARON.

Figure 2. The process of creating artwork by AARON

In 1965, the inventor Ray Kurzweil first composed a piano piece created by a computer that was able to recognize patterns of various musical compositions and use these patterns to create new melodies [14].

B. The second stage

From the end of the 20th century to the beginning of the 21st century is the rising stage of AiArt, that is, the stage of interactive art. The landmark event of this stage was that, in 1997, the "dark blue" robot developed by IBM defeated the world chess champion Kasparov in a competition. Since the 1990s, with the invention of human-computer interaction technologies [15][16], AiArt has gradually separated from previous computer art. The AI system in this period can use sensors and other devices to obtain visual, auditory, and tactile sensations. It can achieve human-computer communication and interaction through receiving information from the surrounding environment (including people), and then use text, voice, motion and other information media and sensor systems to output feedback to users [17]. Artist Char Daives constantly explores the combination and interaction of art and computer graphics. In 1990, he created the first "Interior Body Series" art project based on 3D images. In 1993, he created Osmose (infiltration), which allows visitors to explore the mysteries of the world through operations such as breathing and balance in VR [18].

C. The third stage

From the beginning of the 21st century to now is the stage of popularization of AiArt, that is, the stage of cognitive intelligence art. The landmark event of this stage is that Google-developed robot AlphaGo defeated the world Go champion ninth player Shishi Li by 4: 1 in 2016. Compared with traditional computer programs and systems, AI also has learning and analysis capabilities in addition to perception capabilities, which can adaptively adjust parameters and iteratively optimize models with changes in the environment, tasks, and input data [19]. This means that different inputs result in different effects. Over the past few years, approaches to so-called "Deep Learning", one of the most popular algorithms in AI, have started to produce impressive results by simulating the neurons' construction [20].

In 2015, Some researchers from the University of Tübingen combined realistic pictures with artist styles through using neutrally inspired algorithms [21]. In 2016, Deep Dream, a neural network program first developed by Google, was trained by inputting thousands of pictures for image classification and generating artistic images. The Generative Adversarial Networks (GAN) program was designed to make computers learn and imitate classic artworks in history. In 2017, scientists created a kind of independently creative program Creative Adversarial Networks (CAN) program based on the original GAN, which makes the computer no longer simply emulate the activities of human beings, but create artworks by itself [22].

Artists also use cognitive intelligence to "learn" specific aesthetic rules by analyzing thousands of images, and then try to "create" new images that fit their aesthetic characteristics. Artist Harshit Agrawal of Bangalore based in India, input 60,000 human anatomy pictures into the algorithm, created a series of abstract paintings like crimson blizzards, and finally produced works of art with unique aesthetics of AI. Figure 3 shows "The Anatomy Lesson of Dr. Algorithm" of Harshit Agrawal.

Figure 3. "The Anatomy Lesson of Dr. Algorithm" of Harshit Agrawal (resource: http://harshitagrawal.com/)

This is also how the Portrait of Edmond Belamy, which was sold at a high price in 2018, was created. Three artists from France "feed" thousands of portrait paintings from 500 years ago to the algorithm program, allowing it to "understand" the characteristics of past portrait paintings, so this seemingly weird artwork was created [23].

III. THE ESSENCE OF AIART

The so-called essence is the inherent and intrinsic nature of things. It is the built-in prescriptiveness of a thing that distinguishes it from each other, which makes the world diversified and sophisticated. AiArt is an artistic activity where artists, scientists, engineers, art robots and audiences use AI as the core medium to create, express thoughts and emotions, spreading truth, kindness and beauty. The diversification of subjects, the intelligence of the media, and the modernization of expression are the essence of AiArt, which are the fundamental signs that distinguish AiArt from traditional arts such as painting art, sculpture art, and new media art. Figure 4 explains the block diagram of the essence of AiArt.

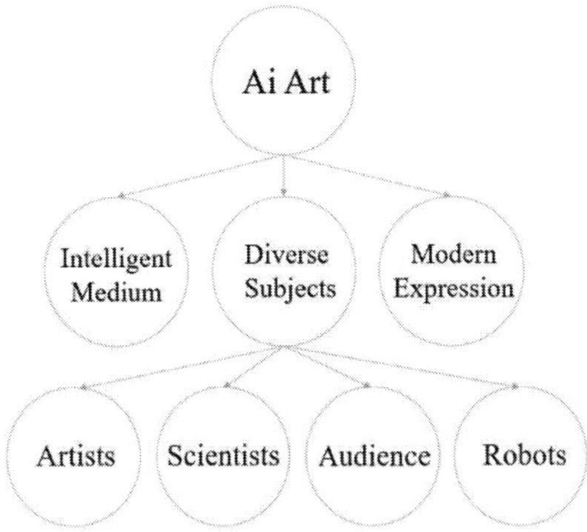

Figure 4. Bolck diagram of the essence of the AiArt

A. The Diversity of Creative Subjects

In the traditional art creation process, the artist who holds the sole right to speak is the only creative subject. With the development of science and technology, the creative power held by the artist is gradually given to the audience and team members [24]. In the creation of AiArt, artists will be limited by the lack of knowledge of AI expertise and technology, which means that not only artists are able to actively cooperate with scientists who grasp the modern scientific knowledge, but that they should form alliances with AI experts to transform algorithms into artistic information. At the same time, with the advance of AI technology, artistic robots have emerged one after another such as painting robots, writing robots, music robots, dance robots, etc. [25]. They can learn, perceive the world like humans, and carry out artistic creation independently which makes them become one of the creative subjects [26]. In AiArt, the audience can also participate in the process of artistic creation and become one of the creators, as the British artist Roy Ascot has profoundly pointed out that art observers who are audiences are no longer just watch the artworks on the sidelines, or from the outside, but can also participate in it and become the central figure in the creative process [27]. AiArt not only opens a window for the audience to understand the world, but also builds a door for the audience, and invites them to enter this interaction and transformation of the digital world. Therefore, the role of the audience in AiArt has undergone a fundamental change that they are no longer spectators in the original sense, but participants and creators. In short, in addition to artists, the creative subjects of AiArt also include scientists, AI experts who work with them and the audience.

B. The Intelligence of the Creative Medium

The form of artistic expression is determined by the feature of the media. As McLuhan said that the difference between old and new art is the difference in the use of media [28]. If the same content is expressed in different media, the effects will be extremely divergent. The media not only determines the way and form of artistic expression but also has a huge impact on the nature and aesthetics of artistic works, which indirectly leads to the changes in artistic thinking and concepts. Compared with traditional media, AI media has unparalleled superiority that it can break away from the constraints of time and space, communicate and interact with the audience in a humane and intelligent way, and integrate the virtual world and reality [29]. In addition to those advantages mentioned above, the intelligent media whose image is intuitive can not only convey a large amount of information faster than before but also have a wider range of transmission, which is easier to be accepted by the audience. At present, AI is widely used in artistic creation, whose core position is becoming increasingly apparent. Although digital AI media is invisible and intangible, it plays a core role in artistic creation that controls the overall context of artworks, reveals the ideological content of the work and replaces part of the artist's labor. This is the value of AI as the core medium.

C. Modernization of Meaning Expression

In the past, traditional artworks are usually stored indoors, and the artist's thoughts and emotions are always hidden in the works, which make the meaning expression passive and indirect. In addition to this, the audience must always keep a certain distance to watch and experience. The meaning expression of AiArt, nevertheless, has special advantages. Not only can the creators' thoughts and emotions be directly expressed through computer vision, speech recognition and sensing technologies, but also break through the constraints of time and space to communicate with the audience through network and remote communication technologies; It also has aesthetic and practical value which could meet people's aesthetic and real needs, and integrates the concept of beauty and artistic style into products. Therefore, AiArt which has various functions like seeking truth, enlightening thinking, and recognizing objective laws can not only entertain people, cultivate sentiment, regulate emotions, but also treat mental illness in the future.

IV. THE CHARACTERISTICS OF AIART

AiArt is a form of art, therefore it has the general characteristics of traditional art, such as creativity, historicity, and aesthetics. However, interaction as a product of the combination of high technology and artistic creation in artistic development will be a new direction for AiArt. It has new features that are different from previous art forms. The new characteristics of AiArt are mainly four aspects: synesthesia experience, flowability and changeability, communication and interaction, and penetration and integration. Figure 5 shows the block diagram of the characteristics of the AiArt.

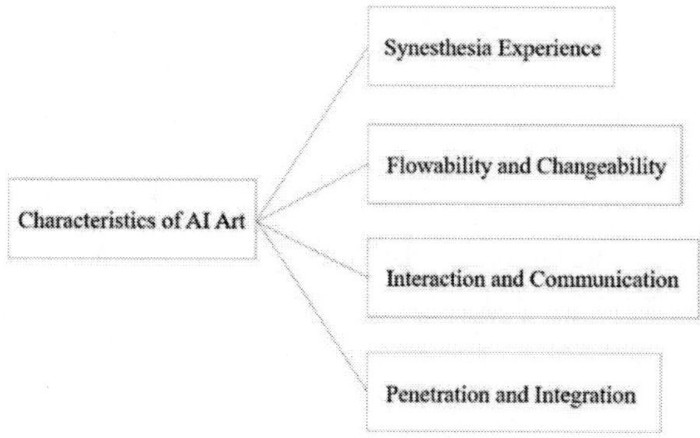

Figure 5. Block diagram of the characteristics of the AiArt

A. Synesthesia Experience

Traditional art is also experiential, but this experience is often single, either a perceptual experience, a visual experience, or an auditory experience that is low-level, superficial, incomplete, and passive. In this experience, the audience's thoughts and emotions about the artworks are incomprehensive, incomplete and superficial. However, the experience of AiArt is full-sense, comprehensive, and omnidirectional. It not only has the perceptual experience, visual experience, and auditory experience but also has a higher level of psychological experience and thinking experience of which the directivity and strong contagiousness can clearly, vividly and comprehensively express the creator's thoughts, emotions and will.

B. Flowability and Changeability

Traditional arts, such as painting, sculpture, and photography are static. They only pay attention to the form and surface but ignore the inner and process of things. However, AiArt that has flowability and changeability is totally different. It reflects the changing process and movement of things. As the British artist, Roy Ascot said that the focus of art has moved from appearance to immanence, which is a dynamic process that moves from the externally visible form to the internal form [27]. AiArt is a kind of infinitely changing art, a flowing art.

C. Interaction and Communication

Interaction and communication are the main features that distinguish AiArt from other art forms. In the future of AiArt, audience can not only interact verbally and physically with artworks, but also communicate spiritually with art creators and participate in the reconstruction of their artworks. This interaction can be audible or silent; it can be direct or indirect; it can be close or long distance. Artists and participants communicate with each other through the AI medium which transforms the audience from the past "viewers" into "participants". This not only means that the creators are able to get rid of the shackles of the spirit, but also makes viewers have a more open, inclusive, and more diverse interpretation of interactive art creation. The AiArt has broken the boundaries between art and life, the subject of creation and the subject of viewing, making Boyce's "social sculpture" ideal of "everyone can be an artist, and everyone is an artist" a reality. Interaction and communication are the new breakthroughs in artistic expression and the new realm of human aesthetic needs, which make AiArt have more prominent advantages and more vitality than traditional art forms.

D. Penetration and Integration

AiArt will be a highly comprehensive cross-media art that not only integrates various elements such as sound, light, video, image and text but also integrates images with exhibition space, virtual space and real space together. What's more important is that it bridges the gap between technology and art, breaks the boundaries between science and art, and opens up a new way for artists to express their thoughts and emotions. With the development of technology, the connected and non-linear integration of AiArt is becoming stronger and stronger, which may become an imperative methodology that could reconcile different or opposite beliefs, and bring different physical and non-physical entity together with philosophy, religion, and cultural customs.

V. CONCLUSION

After the AI was mentioned at the Dartmouth conference in 1956, its technology and content have been changed continually with the progress of the times. Nowadays, it has been given a whole new meaning by big data and deep learning. Therefore, the potential of AI is once again be inspired. And art has been in the process of continuous integration with technology. The combination of AI and art has gone through several stages of development. Only in recent years has it slowly entered the audience's field of vision, and AiArt starts to show an explosive growth trend with various related art exhibitions and competitions followed. However, the theory of AiArt lags behind the practice of creation, and there is a lack of theoretical journals and discussions on the art of AI. This is still a relatively young research area. Based on this, we have identified the need for deeper understanding of how AI and art interact and how they affect and help each other by analyzing and sorting out the context of the development of AiArt.

Here, we have presented the preliminary results of the literature review, showing in which directions research is being done. We have discussed the nature and characteristics of AiArt, which are the most basic and most important thing. It can define AiArt and distinguish it from other art forms through giving this brand-new art genre a label. We believed that the nature of AiArt is determined by three aspects, that is, a diverse creative subject, an intelligent creative medium, and a modern expression of meaning; on the other hand, we also summarized the basic characteristics of AiArt from now to the future: synesthesia experience, flowability and changeability, interaction and communication, penetration and integration.

In the future, we hope we will make a progress by trial and error on theories, models, and tools to explore the potential creativity and innovation in AiArt development.

REFERENCES

[1] G. Torre, "Expectations versus Reality of Artificial Intelligence Using Art to Examine Ontological Issues," Leonardo, Vol. 50, No. 1, pp. 31-35, 2017.

[2] B. A. Y. Arcas. "Art in the Age of Machine Intelligence+," Arts, vol.6, pp. 34-43, Sep. 2017, doi:10.3390/arts6040018.

[3] A. Trifonova, S. U. Ahmed, and L. Jaccheri, "SArt: Towards Innovation at the intersection of Software engineering and art," In Information systems development, pp. 809-827, Boston, MA, 2009.

[4] S. U. Ahmed, C. Camerano, L. Fortuna, M. Frasca, and L. Jaccheri, "Information technology and art: Concepts and state of the practice," In Handbook of Multimedia for Digital Entertainment and Arts, pp. 567-592, Boston, MA, 2009.

[5] P. Kugel, "Artificial Intelligence and Visual Art," Leonardo, vol. 14, pp. 137-139, 1981, doi:10.2307/1574409.

[6] J. Meyer, L. Staples, S. Minneman, M. Naimark, and A. Glassner, "Artists and technologists working together (panel)," In Proceedings of the 11th annual ACM symposium on User interface software and technology, pp. 67-69, Nov. 1998.

[7] S. Wilson, "Computer Art: Artificial Intelligence and the Arts," Leonardo, vol. 16, pp. 15-20, 1983, doi:10.2307/1575036.

[8] K. F. Li and Y. G. Wang, Artificial Intelligence, Beijing: Culture Development Press, pp. 160-217, 2017.

[9] L. Q. Tan, Singularity Art: How Technology Singularity Will Impact Art, Beijing: China Machine Press, pp. 35-72, 2018.

[10] F. Tao, X. H. Zou, and D. Ren, "The Art of Human Intelligence and the Technology of Artificial Intelligence: Artificial Intelligence Visual Art Research," International Conference on Intelligence Science (ICIS 2018), Springer, Cham, Oct. 2018, pp. 146–155, doi: 10.1007/978-3-030-01313-4_15.

[11] P. Machado, J. Romero, A. Santos, A. Cardoso, and A. Pazos, "On the development of evolutionary artificial artists," Computers & Graphics, Vol. 31, pp. 818-826, 2007.

[12] Y. Li, "20 Years of Digital Art," IT Manager World, vol. 495, pp. 68-71, Nov. 2018.

[13] P. Cohen, "Harold Cohen and AARON," Ai Magazine, vol. 37, pp. 63-66, Dec. 2016, doi:10.1609/aimag.v37i4.2695.

[14] H. Barovic, "An Inventive Author," Time International (South Pacific Edition), vol. 156, p. 116, Dec. 2000.

[15] U. S. Ahmed, "Interaction and Interactivity: In the Context of Digital Interactive Art Installation," In International Conference on Human-Computer Interaction, pp. 241-257, July 2018.

[16] U. S. Ahmed, "Developing software-dependent artwork: Artist and software developers' collaboration," Leonardo, Vol.45, pp. 92-93, 2012.

[17] O. H. Cho and W. H. Lee, "Application of Reinforcement Learning System to Interactive Digital Art," Journal of Internet Technology, Vol. 14, pp. 99-106, 2013, doi: 10.6138/JIT.2013.14.1.10.

[18] C. Davies, "OSMOSE: Notes on being in Immersive virtual space," Digital Creativity, vol. 9, pp. 65-74, 1998, doi: 10.1080/14626269808567111.

[19] M. Mateas, "Expressive AI: A Hybrid Art and Science Practice," Leonardo, vol. 34, No. 2, pp. 147–153, 2001, doi: 10.1162/002409401750184717.

[20] I. Goodfellow, Y. Bengio, and A. Courville, Deep Learning, Boston: MIT Press, pp.24-108, 2016.

[21] L. A. Gatys, A. S. Ecker, and M. Bethge, "A Neural Algorithm of Artistic Style," Journal of Vision, vol. 16, pp. 326, Sep. 2016, doi:https://doi.org/10.1167/16.12.326

[22] A. Elgammal, B. Liu, M. Elhoseiny, and M. Mazzone. "CAN: Creative Adversarial Networks Generating 'Art' by Learning About Styles and Deviating from Style Norms," the Eighth International Conference on Computational Creativity (ICCC), pp.1-22, 2017.

[23] S. M. Du, "Can AI ever be truly creative?" New Scientist, vol. 242, pp.38-41, Nov. 2019, doi:10.1016/S0262-4079(19)30840-1.

[24] D. F. Albertini, "From artefactual to artificial intelligence—meeting the needs of ART patients and practitioners," Journal of Assisted Reproduction and Genetics, vol. 35, pp. 1543–1544, 2018.

[25] G. W. Smith and F. F. Leymarie, "The Machine as Artist: An Introduction," Arts, vol.6, pp.28-35, April 2017, doi:10.3390/arts6020005.

[26] M. Shidujaman and H. Mi, "Which Country Are You from? A Cross-Cultural Study on Greeting Interaction Design for Social Robots, " In International Conference on Cross-Cultural Design, pp. 362-374, Springer, Cham, July. 2018.

[27] R. Ascott, The Future is Now: Art, Technology and Consciousness, Beijing: Jincheng Press, pp. 1–278, 2012.

[28] H. M. Mcluhan, Understanding the Media: An Extension of the Man, Beijing: Commercial Press, pp. 46–326, 2000.

[29] A. Lomas, "On Hybrid Creativity," Arts, vol.7,pp.38-48, 2018, doi:10.3390/arts7030025.

A non-Invasive Approach to Extract the User's Patterns of Visual Arts Exploration through Wearable Technologies Application: the NEFFIE Project

Diana Trojaniello, Matteo Zardin, Marco Mura, Alberto Sanna
Center for Advanced Technology in Health and Wellbeing
IRCSS San Raffaele Hospital
Milan, Italy
e-mail: trojaniello.diana@hsr.it, zardin.matteo@hsr.it, mura.marco@hsr.it, sanna.alberto@hsr.it

Abstract— **Understanding human cognitive perception processes during visual art fruition represents both a neuroscientific and technological challenge. By addressing the cognitive processes behind the art appreciation and by employing the last generation technologies to analyze human bio signals, the NEFFIE project aims to propose a new approach to emphasize the visual art fruition experience while increasing the awareness of what we actually see. The project consists of four different experimental phases, including both In-Lab and Out-Lab evaluations: I) In-Lab images rating; II) In-Lab functional Magnetic Resonance Imaging fMRI -based study; III) In-Lab Wearable-based study; IV) Out-Lab Wearable-based study. Through these experimental steps, the NEFFIE project will develop a unique platform based on Artificial Intelligence human-centric algorithms to identify each person's unique fingerprint of visual art perception and discovery. The current idea-paper aims to describe the above-mentioned experimental phases.**

Keywords - visual art; wearable; fMRI; artificial intelligence; machine learning.

I. INTRODUCTION

In literature, Visual Arts (VAs) including paintings, sculptures and photography have been always defined as an aesthetic expression of interiority and of the human soul. VAs reflect the artist's opinions, feelings and thoughts in the social, moral, cultural, ethical and religious context of his historical period. Philosophers and semantic scholars, however, argue that an objective language exists that, regardless of the eras and styles, should be codified in order to be understood by everyone, but so far efforts to demonstrate this claim have been found unsuccessful.

Thanks to the technology advancements, nowadays it is possible to understand more precisely how the subjective process of aesthetic appreciation of VA forms takes place. Recent studies showed that "aesthetic experience" involves brain areas devoted to different functions [1], such as the body representation and its movements, and the analysis of the hedonic value of perceived stimuli. The above-mentioned brain areas are activated automatically when people observe VA forms, even if they have not been asked to judge them critically. Functional Magnetic Resonance Imaging (fMRI) allow to identify the brain areas associated with the aesthetic experience.

However, such an in-depth study has physical and non-physical limits, e.g., the impossibility to present images for a longer time interval, necessary for the observer to ensure deep contemplation. This is why new technologies and sensors (i.e., wearable devices able to monitor physiological signals) could be employed to monitor physiological parameters in un-constrained environments thus allowing a longer VA form fruition in a quasi-real life context.

Monitoring methods such as ElectroEncephaloGraphy (EEG), Eye-Tracking (ET), Face Recognition (FR). PhotoPletismoGraphy (PPG) and Galvanic Skin Response registration (GSR) allow to collect physiological data highly correlated with the brain activity and emotions through wearable devices mounted on the subjects [2]. For example, the usage of such methods through an integrated multi-sensors platform allow to register the electrical activity produced by populations of neurons on the observer cerebral cortex (EEG), while detecting eye movements and fixation points (ET), to identify which aspects of the VA form capture the attention of the observer and reach his consciousness. In addition, by including the emotions as expressed by the face (FR) and electro dermal activity variation (GSR) it is possible to detect the emotional activation level of the observer.

The NEFFIE project will develop a unique multi-sensors platform based on Artificial Intelligence (AI) human-centric algorithms to identify each person's unique fingerprint of visual art perception and discovery in un-constrained environments. The current idea-paper aims to describe the experimental activities flow that will allow to develop the NEFFIE platform. The paper is organized as following: in Section I the introduction has been reported; in Section II the project experimental phases have been described; in Section III conclusion and future works have been reported.

II. PROJECT EXPERIMENTAL PHASES

In the following sections (A, B, C, D), the four experimental phases of the NEFFIE project (In-Lab images rating, In-Lab fMRI based study, In-Lab Wearable based study, Out-Lab Wearable based study) have been briefly described.

A. *In-Lab images rating*

The first phase of the project consisted in an *image (photo) rating study*. A total of 218 images have been collected and divided in two groups of images, i.e., Neffie Group (N-G) and Control Group (C-G). The N-G images were characterized by an high presence of reflections and in general complex elements, while the C-G ones were characterized by a simpler content. Eighty healthy subjects have been included in the study and divided into 4 groups. Each group was asked to rate on a 7-points Likert scale the 218 images, presented in a random way, with respect to one of the four following dimensions: a) presence of reflections; b) complexity; c) beauty; d) stimulating. The results obtained in this first study allowed to identify a sub-set of images (n=61) characterized by higher levels of complexity and able to arouse the observer.

B. *In-Lab fMRI-based study*

The second phase of the project consisted in a *fMRI based study*. The study has been designed on the basis of the results obtained in the previous phase by including the subset of 61 images identified in the *In-Lab image rating study*. Thirty-six healthy subjects will take part to the study and will be invited to receive a fMRI evaluation while observing the 61 N-G images and 61 C-G matched ones. The main objective of this phase is to evaluate the BOLD signal variation through the fMRI technique in those brain area involved in the complex visual stimuli analysis (N-G images). In general, this phase of the project aims to establish a relation between the brain activity and the aesthetic experience of the subject while observing N-G and C-G images. In addition, the eye-tracking technique will be employed to measure the fixation points and the image area, which is more involved in the visual exploratory pattern of the subject. This study will start in the first part of 2020.

C. *In-Lab Wearable-based study*

The second phase of the project consisted in a *wearable sensors based study* performed in-lab environment under the supervision of a researcher. The main objective of this phase was to identify the minimum viable number of sensors able to describe in the most accurate way the aesthetic experience (i.e., emotion level through valence and arousal levels identification) of the subject while observing a VA form. A multi sensors platform has been developed including the following devices: EEG, ET, GSR and PhotoPletismoGraphy PPG. The platform allowed the researchers to register the subjects bio-signals synchronized with the visualization of a number of images extracted by the Nencki Affective Picture System (NAPS) database.

Figure 1. The In-Lab Wearable based study experimental setup.

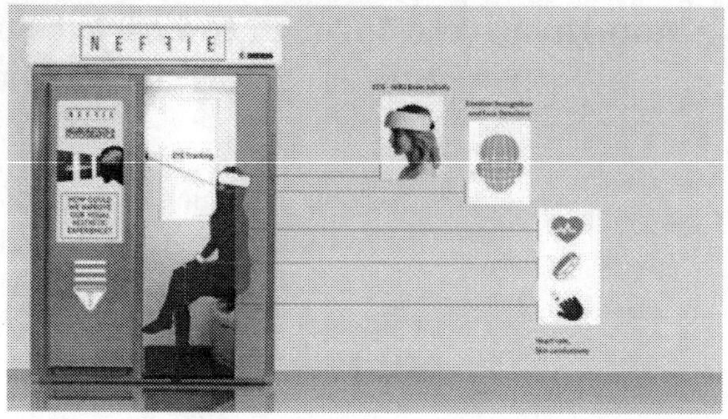

Figure 2. The Out-Lab Wearable based study experimental setup.

Forty-three subjects have been enrolled in this study. Bio-signals were recorded during the presentation of visual stimuli (baseline image, eliciting image) from NAPS, which were at the same time evaluated by the subjects (self-reports on arousal, valence and emotional label). Figure 2 shows the experimental setup adopted for the experiment. AI algorithms including Neural Networks and Support Vector Machines have been then applied in order to find the most accurate one to identify arousal and valence levels (i.e., with respect to the reference values associated to each image as reported in the NAPS database).

D. *Out-Lab Wearable-based study*

The last phase of the project consisted in the application of the previous phase in an un-constrained environment. The same setup as developed and used in the *In-Lab wearable based study phase* has been placed inside a photo booth provided by an external company (as shown in Figure 3). The photo boot has been equipped with a touch screen. The subjects will be invited to enter in the photo booth and to wear the wearable devices placed inside and then to start the experiment. A set of images among those 61 ones selected in the *image rating study* will be presented on the screen while the subject bio-signals will be registered. Once the image presentation will be concluded, the subject will be requested to choose among one of them to be printed. The printed image will be the reinterpretation of the observed image on the basis of the bio signals registered and analyzed.

This study will start in March 2020.

III. Conclusions and Future Works

The present paper outlines the current experimental phases of the NEFFIE project. The In-Lab fMRI as well as the Out-Lab Wearable based studies will start in the first half of 2020.

References

[1] G. Udovičić, J. Đerek, M. Russo, and M. Sikora. 2017. Wearable Emotion Recognition System based on GSR and PPG Signals. In Proceedings of the 2nd International Workshop on Multimedia for Personal Health and Health Care.

[2] E. Vessel, G.G. Starr, N. Rubin, 2012. The brain on art: intense aesthetic experience activates the default mode network Front Hum Neurosci. 2012; 6: 66.

International Academy, Research,
and Industry Association (IARIA)
412 Derby Way
Wilmington, DE 19810

ISBN 978-1-7138-1210-4

CURRAN ASSOCIATES INC.
proceedings.com

Twelfth International Conference on Advances in Semantic Processing (SEMAPRO 2018)

Held at NexTech 2018

Athens, Greece
18-22 November 2018

IARIA